The Logic of Common Nouns

The Logic of Common Nouns

An Investigation in Quantified Modal Logic

Anil Gupta

New Haven and London
Yale University Press
1980

Designed by Sally Harris
and set in Times Roman type.
Printed in the United States of America.

Library of Congress Cataloging in Publication Data

Gupta, Anil.
The logic of common nouns.

Bibliography: p.
Includes index.
1. Modality (Logic) I. Title.
BC199.M6G86 1980 160 79-19684
ISBN 0-300-02346-4

1 2 3 4 5 6 7 8 9 10

To
my mother
Pushpa Wati Jain
and my father
Desh Raj Gupta

Contents

Preface

My aim in this essay is to explore the logical role of an important class of concepts—concepts that are expressed by common nouns ("sortal concepts")—in a fragment of our conceptual scheme. It seems to me that this exploration is essential not only for purely logical purposes but for certain philosophical and linguistic purposes as well. The logic of common nouns, I believe, illuminates and helps solve the problem of essentialism. It explains some of the distinctive behavior of common nouns in our language. And it provides material that I think will lead to a better understanding of the relationship of logic to ontology, the behavior of mass nouns, and the vagueness in singular terms. Although in many ways my discussion of these topics is incomplete, I am convinced of the relevance of the logic of common nouns to important issues in philosophy and linguistics. I hope that philosophers and linguists will not let their natural aversion to technical logic turn them away from this work.

I should note that not much technical background is necessary to follow the main arguments in this essay: familiarity with the rudiments of modal logic (roughly the material covered in chapters 1–5 and 8–11 of Hughes and Cresswell (1968)) is sufficient. All of the very technical parts may be skipped by readers not interested in formal details. In particular, chapter 1, §9, chapter 2, and chapter 5, §§4 and 5, may be omitted without loss of continuity. It is essential, however, to grasp the definition of truth given in chapter 1, §7. It is crucial to all that follows.

This essay is a slightly revised version of my doctoral dissertation submitted to the University of Pittsburgh in April 1977. The ideas presented here were first developed in my seminar on modal logic given at McGill University in the fall of 1975.

McGill University, Montreal Anil Gupta

Acknowledgments

I wish to acknowledge a deep and profound debt to my teachers Professors Nuel Belnap and Richmond Thomason. Every idea put forward here has its origin in something they said first, and every formulation has benefited considerably from their patient scrutiny. I am especially indebted to Nuel Belnap for chapters 1–3. His lectures on Bressan, given in fall 1970 and summer 1973 at the University of Pittsburgh, greatly influenced my ideas about common nouns. For chapters 3–5 I am greatly indebted to Richmond Thomason. My remarks on Davidson's semantic program and the concept of truth, in particular, owe much to the numerous discussions we had on the subject and also to his paper "Necessity, Quotation and Truth" (1976).

I have also benefited from discussions with a number of friends. I would like to thank especially Molly Conway, Steven Davis, Allan Gibbard, John Hawthorn, Allen Hazen, Christopher Hill, Robert Kraut, Storrs McCall, James McGilvray, and Emanuel Schorsch.

Finally, thanks are due to McGill University for a Humanities Research Grant which helped meet the costs of preparing the final draft and to D. Reidel Publishing Company for permission to use those parts of chapter 5 which appeared in the *Journal of Philosophical Logic*, volume 7, number 4.

Introduction

I argue that there are important logical and semantic differences between common nouns and predicates, and I construct systems of quantified modal logic that reflect these differences (chapters 1–3). In the last two chapters (chapters 4 and 5), I defend the systems offered against two important objections to modal logic found in the literature. This introduction presents and motivates, in an informal and simplified way, some of the key ideas developed rigorously in the following chapters.

According to the standard theory, familiar from extensional and modal logics, there are no significant logical or semantic differences between common nouns and predicates. In these logics, categorematic expressions are divided into two fundamental classes: *singular term* and *predicate*. Names, definite descriptions, and other terms that refer (or purport to refer) to just one object belong to the logical category of singular term; common nouns, adjectives, verbs,[1] and other expressions that combine with singular terms to yield sentences belong to the logical category of predicate. Thus, according to the standard account, common nouns, adjectives, verbs, etc., have, despite differences in their grammatical behavior, the same semantic role. As the standard account views it, the multiplicity of grammatical roles does not point to any multiplicity of semantic roles.[2] (This view is elaborated and defended in Quine (1960), among other places.) My aim is to argue that there is more to the logical and semantic behavior of common nouns than is captured in the standard theory.

Common nouns, like predicates, are true or false of objects. They

1. In some accounts (e.g., Davidson's) adverbs are also included in this list.

2. The standard treatment of adjectives has been criticized by Montague and others. But these authors follow the standard theory in assimilating common nouns and intransitive verbs in one logical category. Montague (1974), for example, makes a syntactic distinction between common nouns and intransitive verbs but makes no distinction in their semantic interpretations.

divide all the objects in the world into two classes: those objects that fall under them, and those that do not. That is, common nouns, like predicates, supply a *principle of application.* This principle determines the extension of the common noun, or the predicate, at each world (and time). But, as Geach has noted, common nouns, unlike predicates, also supply a *principle of identity.* A common noun, such as 'river', provides a rule that determines when an object at a time (and a world) is *the same river* as an object at another time (and a world). I should emphasize that I do not understand 'principle of identity' in an epistemic way. I do not mean by it a rule or a principle that the speaker of a language tacitly *knows.* It is not the rule by which one *determines,* say, when an object is the same river as another object. It is rather the metaphysical counterpart of such an epistemic rule. The principle of identity for 'river' is the rule *in virtue of which* an object at a time (and a world) is the same river as an object at another time (and a world).

I argue (in chapter 1, §5) that an adequate theory of the intensions of common nouns must represent both the principles of identity and the principles of application. Standard systems of quantified modal logic fail in this respect. Here the intensions of common nouns and (one-place) predicates are represented by *properties,* which are functions from possible worlds to sets of individuals. But properties represent only the principle of application associated with a term. Hence, although properties are a good representation of the intensions of predicates, they are not adequate as representations of the intensions of common nouns. They fail to represent the principles of identity. Equivalently, they treat all common nouns as supplying the same principle of identity. In either case the standard theory is unacceptable. Or so I argue in chapter 1, §5.

But how *are* the intensions of common nouns, and in particular their principles of identity, to be represented? The semantics of modal logic interprets the singular terms and the predicates relative to some specification of the domains of the various possible worlds. Thus we find in the semantics two components. The first component is the model structure; this specifies the worlds and their domains. The second component is the valuation; this gives the interpretation of the singular terms and predicates relative to a fixed model structure. But it seems that the identity of a thing—for example a ship—in the various possible worlds is determined entirely by the model structure. For we are tempted to say that a ship d, for example, in a world w is the same ship as a ship d′ in a world w′ if and only if d = d′. On this view, however, the interpretation of a common noun can represent only its principle of application; the principles of identity are fixed by the model structure. We are back to the standard theory.

Thus one major problem that needs to be solved is this: how are the intensions of common nouns to be represented in modal logic? If we call the intensions of common nouns 'sorts' (in the manner that the intensions of sentences are called 'propositions', and those of predicates 'properties' or 'relations'), then the question is: what are sorts? How are they to be understood in the model theory of modal logics?

My suggestion for the solution of this problem is that we should not take trans-world identities of objects to be fixed and given at the start by the model structures. Rather, we should let these identities be determined by the interpretations of common nouns. There will, of course, be a favored concept of trans-world identity in the metalanguage (namely, that expressed by the metalinguistic '='), but this concept does not affect the interpretation of the object language sentences. In formal terms this means that changes in the trans-world identities in the metalanguage leave the truth values of the object language sentences unchanged. More picturesquely, the point is this: in the interpretation of the object language it does not matter how the metalanguage carves the world into objects.

This suggestion motivates one of the key ideas developed below, namely, that sorts are (or, more accurately, are represented by) certain kinds of *intensional properties*. An intensional property is a function that yields a set of individual concepts at each world. (Individual concepts in turn are functions that yield an individual at each world.) Individual concepts falling under a sort, say 'ship' trace *particular* ships from world to world (and moment to moment). A collection of such individual concepts represents the principle of identity for 'ship'. Note that individual concepts falling under a sort may vary from world to world. The reasons for this are given in chapter 1, §5. Note also that not all intensional properties represent sorts. I explore at length what other conditions need to be fulfilled by intensional properties. The first proposal, offered in chapter 1, is based on the simplifying supposition that common nouns pick out necessary existents—if an instance of a common noun *K* exists in one world, it exists in all the worlds. The theory is generalized in chapter 3 to take into account possible non-existence. A final generalization occurs in chapter 4. This is motivated by certain distinctive properties of terms for artifacts and assemblies.

I construct systems of quantified modal logic in which a categorial distinction is made between common nouns and predicates. The syntactic and semantic behavior of common nouns in these logics is quite different from the behavior of predicates. Syntactically, common nouns combine with quantifiers, variables, and formulas to yield formulas, but predicates do not. Semantically, common nouns express sorts, but predicates express properties. These ideas are interrelated in the following way. I argue that a variable needs to have associated with it not only an object but also a principle of identity that traces the value of the variable from world to world. This principle of identity is just what is supplied by the common noun connected with the quantifier. Thus the semantic fact that common nouns (but not predicates) express a principle of identity is reflected in the syntactic fact that only common nouns combine with quantifiers and variables.

I offer a variety of modal systems. Some of the differences between these systems are due to the different theories of sorts on which they are based. Other differences are due to the way nonexistence is treated in the semantics of necessity. All systems have the following two distinctive features. First, identity is contingent in these systems. Schema (1) is invalid,

(1) $s = t \supset \Box s = t$,

even when the terms *s* and *t* are variables (see chapter 1, §9). Second, Fregean analyses fail in our systems. That is, sentences such as

(2) Every *K* is *F*,
(3) Some *K* is *F*

are not in general equivalent to

(4) Everything is such that if it is a *K*, then it is *F*,
(5) Something is such that it is a *K* and it is *F*,

respectively. Thus "sortal quantification" is not eliminable in favor of unrestricted quantification. Our systems are not notational variants of the standard systems. In fact, standard systems can be viewed as special cases of systems offered here: standard systems, it can be said, have sortal quantification but they countenance just one common noun, 'thing'. (See chapter 4, §1, for a discussion of unrestricted quantification and the noun 'thing'. See also chapter 1, §5.)

In the last two chapters I examine and answer two major objections to modal logics. The first objection, raised by Quine, is that quantified modal logics are committed to an unacceptable essentialism. I consider this objection in chapter 4. I show that the essentialistic commitments of modal logics presented in chapters 1–3 are considerably weaker than the essentialistic commitments of the standard systems. And I argue that the weaker kind of essentialism is unobjectionable. In this connection I examine in detail a problem about essentialism and trans-world identity which was raised by Chisholm in 1967. I suggest that Chisholm's problem is generated by a plausible but false assumption about common nouns.

According to the second objection, put forward by Davidson and by Wallace, quantified modal logics fail to meet Tarski's convention T. Davidson and Harman have argued, and Wallace has agreed, that convention T imposes a reasonable adequacy condition on logics. Wallace has argued, and Davidson and Harman have agreed, that quantified modal logics fail to satisfy Tarski's convention. (This is somewhat simplified. For a more accurate account see chapter 5.) I show that Wallace's argument is easily refuted once we distinguish two concepts of truth, and I construct theories of truth *in* modal logics which fulfill convention T. Thus Wallace's claim is seen to be false. I also suggest that we should not accept Davidson's adequacy condition on logics. (My argument here is less conclusive.) Finally I offer Davidson-style (i.e., "truth-theoretic" as opposed to "model-theoretic") semantics for various modal languages, including a modal language with sortal quantification.

1 The Logic of Common Nouns: The Language L_1

The modal language L_1 presented in this chapter has, besides the usual logical categories, *predicate*, *singular term*, *variable*, and *sentence*, an additional logical category, the *common noun*. This is perhaps the most distinctive feature of L_1. Unlike standard logics, both extensional and modal, predicates and common nouns are treated differently in L_1. Syntactically, common nouns of L_1 combine with quantifiers, variables, and formulas to yield formulas. They combine with relative clauses to yield compound common nouns, and they combine with the description operator, ℩ ('the'), to form singular terms. Predicates engage in no such behavior. On the other hand, common nouns of L_1 never occur in predicative positions. The significant differences between common nouns and predicates, however, are semantic rather than syntactic. The semantic values of common nouns and predicates in L_1 are quite different—and indeed some of these differences are used to explain the differences in their syntactic behavior.

Part I (§§1, 2) presents the syntax of L_1 with some informal remarks to relate the constructions of L_1 to constructions of English. In part II (especially §§3–8) I present the semantics of L_1. Section 9 discusses some valid and some invalid formulas of L_1. Section 10 records some useful metatheorems concerning the semantics of L_1. This last section may be skipped by readers not interested in formal details.

PART I

The Syntax of L_1

§1. Rules of Formation, etc.

The basic nonlogical symbols of L_1 are divided into these categories: *individual constant*, *variable*, *n-place predicate*, and *atomic common noun*. L_1 has at most denumerably many individual constants, predicates, and atomic common nouns. The category of individual constants may be empty, but L_1 has at least one predicate and one atomic common noun. Further, L_1 has denumerably many variables. We suppose for convenience that the symbols of all the categories are ordered.[1]

The logical symbols of L_1 are $=$, $\sim$, $\supset$, $\Box$, $\forall$, and ℩. We define by simultaneous recursion the notions of *term*, *common noun*, and *formula*.

Definition 1

(i) All individual constants and variables are *terms* and more specifically *atomic terms*.

(ii) All atomic common nouns are *common nouns*.

(iii) If s and t are terms, then $s = t$ is a *formula*—more specifically an *atomic formula*.

(iv) If F is an n-place predicate and $t_1, \ldots, t_n$ are terms, then $F(t_1, \ldots, t_n)$ is a formula (also an atomic formula).

(v) If A and B are formulas, then so are $\sim A$, $\Box A$, and $(A \supset B)$.

(vi) If K is a common noun, x is a variable, and A is a formula, then $(\forall K,x)A$ is a formula.

(vii) If K is a common noun, x a variable, and A a formula, then $(K,x)A$ is a common noun.

(viii) If K is a common noun, then ℩K is a term.[2]

1. L_1, then, can be identified with a quadruple ⟨IC, V, Pred, CN⟩ which satisfies the following requirements: (i) IC is a sequence of symbols, possibly empty but at most denumerable; (ii) V is a denumerable sequence of symbols; (iii) Pred is a denumerable sequence of at most denumerable sequences—at least one sequence belonging to Pred is required to be nonempty; (iv) CN is a sequence of symbols at least nonempty but at most denumerable; (v) all sequences are "disjoint" and no item is repeated within a sequence. Given a language L_1 we can easily define purely syntactic concepts such as that of an n-place predicate.

In this and the following chapters I shall often speak as though L_1 is a specific language and present some results that hold for L_1; but this is merely an expository convenience. I am really describing languages of a certain kind, and the results presented for L_1 hold for all languages of that kind.

2. A note on the metalinguistic conventions followed in this essay. I use *italicized* symbols 't', 't'', 's', ..., as metalinguistic variables ranging over terms of L_1; 'x', 'y', 'x'', ..., as ranging over variables; 'a', 'b', 'c', 'a'', ..., over individual constants; 'F', 'G', 'F'', 'F_1', ..., over predicates; 'K', 'K'' over common nouns; 'A', 'B', 'C', 'A'', ..., over formulas; and the greek letters 'α', 'β', ..., over expressions (defined below); 'Γ', 'Δ' over sets of formulas. I use *bold italicized* versions of these symbols to represent constants of the corresponding category. (For the most part I have followed the conventions of Anderson and Belnap's *Entailment* (1975).)

We understand the familiar syntactic notions such as "free occurrence of a variable in a formula (or a term or a common noun)" defined as usual. In particular, by an *expression* we understand any string that is either a term or a common noun or a formula. An expression is *closed* if it has no free occurrences of a variable. A *theory* is a set of closed formulas. A term t *occurs* in a set of formulas Γ iff t occurs in a member of Γ. A variable x is *free* in a set of formulas Γ iff x is free in a member of Γ. A set of formulas is *modally closed* iff all its members are of the form $\Box A$ or $\sim \Box A$.

We represent by 'α^t/x' the expression that results when the term t is substituted for all the free occurrences of x in α. We introduce by metalinguistic definitions the familiar logical connectives $\vee$, $\wedge$, $\equiv$, $\Diamond$, $\exists$, and $\exists!$.

Definition 2

(i) $(A \vee B) = \text{Df}((A \supset B) \supset B)$.

(ii) $(A \wedge B) = \text{Df} \sim (A \supset \sim B)$.

(iii) $(A \equiv B) = \text{Df}((A \supset B) \wedge (B \supset A))$.

(iv) $\Diamond A = \text{Df} \sim \Box \sim A$.

(v) $(\exists K,x)A = \text{Df} \sim (\forall K,x) \sim A$.

(vi) $(\exists !K,x)A = \text{Df}(\exists K,y)(\forall K,x)(A \equiv x = y)$, where y is the first variable distinct from x which does not occur in A or in K.

Finally, we often omit and sometimes add parentheses when this can cause no ambiguity or confusion. The conventions for omitting parentheses are standard (see, for instance, Leblanc and Wisdom (1974)).

§2. *Informal Remarks*

In English, the expressions that count as common nouns are a heterogeneous bunch. They can be simple ('animal') or complex ('artificial limb').[3] Some common nouns divide their reference; some do not ('water').[4] Some are true of ordinary things ('table', 'tree'); others are true of stranger entities such as events ('walk'), abstract objects ('set'), and intensional objects ('color'). Some common nouns give essential properties of objects ('horse'), others merely accidental

3. For an explanation of this deviation from standard grammar see the fourth paragraph below.

4. Common nouns include both mass nouns and count nouns.

ones ('student'). A fuller logic of common nouns would draw these and other distinctions. The logic presented here displays their shared features.

Common nouns share several semantic and syntactic properties of interest to logic. For example, common nouns are proper responses to certain types of "What?" questions. They are used to pick out and to classify objects. Syntactically, common nouns combine with quantifiers and other determiners to form noun phrases. And quantifiers (and determiners) rarely occur in complete sentences without common nouns.[5] This syntactic feature I explain below on the basis of the semantics of variables and common nouns. It turns out that variables make sense only if a certain type of information is supplied, and this information is carried distinctively by common nouns (and by proper names). This leads me to propose the following hypothesis.

Hypothesis. Wherever there is variable binding (or its analogue) in the syntax of a language, there is also a common noun (or a proper name) binding the variable (or its analogue).[6]

I have noted that one mark of common nouns is that they combine with quantifiers. But not all expressions found with quantifiers are common nouns. An important exception is lists of proper names. As Geach (1962) has observed, lists of proper names such as 'one of John, Fred, and Mary' or 'of John, Fred, and Mary' can often be substituted for common nouns *salva congruitate*—the former when the common noun is in the singular, the latter when it is in the plural. We may be tempted to treat these lists as common nouns. The temptation should be resisted: there are semantic arguments against such a treatment (see p. 35).

5. A few qualifications. First, the common noun may not occur in the sentence physically, but it may be understood from the context of use. Second, the sentence may contain implicit quantification over common noun positions as in 'Whatever Mary likes, Jim likes'. And third, when the quantifier is understood substitutionally, it need not be accompanied by a common noun. (I am inclined to give a substitutional interpretation to a quantifier when it is followed by a list of proper names.)

6. All the qualifications mentioned in note 5, of course, apply. A further qualification concerns variables that occur in positions not occupied by singular terms. The hypothesis is not meant to apply to these unless they are mere surface manifestations of variables in singular terms positions (i.e., pronouns) in the deep or logical structure.

Compound expressions such as

(1) Man who likes Margaret

also combine with quantifiers, and I include them in the category of common nouns. Here again, I depart from traditional grammar. Such compound expressions are not usually thought of as common nouns. However, the logic, and in many ways the syntax, of such expressions is so close to the logic and syntax of common nouns, so-called, that I see no special need to justify this departure from traditional grammar.[7] Grammar, after all, is only a guide for logic, not a substitute.

Language L_1 has a device that allows the formation of compound common nouns from simpler ones. A common noun K combines with a variable x and a sentence A to yield the common noun $(K,x)A$ (Definition 1(vii)). I call this operation *restriction*. The restricted common nouns of L_1 represent compound common nouns of English, such as (1). This is represented in L_1 by

(2) $(M,x)Lxm$,

where M stands for 'man', L for the two-place predicate 'likes', and m for 'Margaret'.

The operation of restriction resembles the operation of λ-abstraction familiar from standard logic. But there are important differences. The operation λ-abstraction yields predicates. Restriction, on the other hand, yields common nouns. There is an exact correspondence between English common nouns and restricted common nouns. Expression (1) is an exact translation of (2). With λ-abstraction the correspondence with natural languages is not so close. For instance,

(3) $\lambda xLxm$

cannot be read as 'thing that likes Margaret', nor as 'liking Margaret', for neither is a predicate. The closest expression in English that translates (3) is the tortuous 'is such that it likes Margaret', or the equally tortuous 'is a thing that likes Margaret'.

Geach has argued that expressions such as 'man who likes Margaret' are not proper logical units. If he is right, then (2) and expressions like

7. Surprisingly, there is no standard name for the category of expressions I am calling "common nouns." Stockwell, Schachter, and Partee (1973) call them "nominals," but there is no general acceptance of their usage. Cresswell, for example, uses "nominals" to designate noun phrases.

it should not be treated as belonging to the logical category of common nouns. Geach begins his argument for this by observing that the English sentence (4) is properly paraphrased as (5):

(4) Any animal that can bray is a donkey,

(5) Any animal, *if he* can bray, is a donkey;

whereas (6) is properly paraphrased as (7):

(6) Socrates is an animal that can bray,

(7) Socrates is an animal *and he* can bray.

Now note that in the context 'Any ——— is a donkey', the common noun 'animal that can bray' is replaceable by 'animal, if he can bray' *salva significatione*, whereas it is not so replaceable in the context 'Socrates is an ———'. This suggests to Geach that the phrase 'animal that can bray' is ambiguous—meaning in one context 'animal, *if he* can bray' and in another 'animal, *and he* can bray'. Further, since neither of the last two expressions is a proper logical unit, Geach suggests that 'animal that can bray' is not a proper logical unit either (Geach (1962) pp. 115–19). Geach recognizes that this argument is untrustworthy. It commits a fallacy that Geach has called "canceling out fallacy." But he continues, "We may however confirm the suggestion of ambiguity by considering another sort of medieval example." Geach considers the sentences

(8) Any man who owns a donkey beats it,

(9) Some man who owns a donkey does not beat it.

He rightly observes that 'man who owns a donkey' is not a proper logical unit in these two sentences and that it does not mean 'donkey-owner'. But, even granting that 'man who owns a donkey' is ambiguous—meaning one thing in (8) and another in (9)—how does this confirm the ambiguity of restricted common nouns claimed above? How does this show that 'man who owns a donkey' means 'man, *if he* owns a donkey' in one context and 'man *and he* owns a donkey' in another? This conclusion does not follow unless the canceling out fallacy is committed again. (Even with the canceling out fallacy, the conclusion does not seem to follow—consider Geach's (18) and (19), p. 118.)

'Man who owns a donkey' is not a proper logical unit in (8) and (9). But this should not be taken to show that restricted common nouns are not logical units. Such an argument, if allowed, can be used to show that sentences are not proper logical units either. It is easily seen that

(10) Some man owns a donkey

cannot be treated as a logical unit in

(11) Some man owns a donkey and beats it.

However, we should not conclude that 'Some man owns a donkey' is *never* a proper logical unit—that sentences are a "logical mirage." The proper conclusion is that (10) does not have a genuine occurrence in (11). Superficially, it is a part of it, but it is not a part from the logical viewpoint. Similarly, 'man who owns a donkey' does not have a genuine occurrence in (8) and (9). As with (11), the problem is caused by the scope of the phrase 'a donkey'. Propositions (8) and (9) are represented in L_1 by

(12) $(\forall D,x)(\forall(M,y)Oyx,z)Bzx$,

(13) $(\exists D,x)(\exists(M,y)Oyx,z) \sim Bzx$,

respectively, where D stands for 'donkey', M for 'man', O for 'owns', and B for 'beats'. Clearly, the expression

$(M,y)(\exists D,x)Oyx$,

which represents 'man who owns a donkey', does not occur in (12) and (13).

Sentence (8) can also be represented in L_1 by

(14) $(\forall D,x)(\forall M,y)(Oyx \supset Byx)$.

In general, sentences

(15) Any K that is F is G,[8]

(16) Some K that is F is G

can be represented in L_1 either as

(17) $(\forall(K,x)Fx,y)Gy$,

(18) $(\exists(K,x)Fx,y)Gy$,

or as

(19) $(\forall K,x)(Fx \supset Gx)$,

(20) $(\exists K,x)(Fx \wedge Gx)$,

respectively. Thus (15) and (16) can be paraphrased as

(21) Every K is such that if it is F, it is G,

(22) Some K is F and G.

8. I ignore use–mention difficulties. Variables 'K', 'F', 'G', 't', etc., in contexts such as this are to be understood substitutionally.

Classical logic and semantics carry this analysis one step further and one step too far. Sentence (21) and (22) are further analyzed as

(23) Any*thing*, if it is a K and if it is F, is G,

(24) Some*thing* is a K and F and G.

It will be shown later that (21) and (22) are not in general equivalent to (23) and (24). They are equivalent only under some very strong ontological assumptions which, I shall argue, we should not make. Thus I hold that the common nouns 'man' and 'thing that is a man' are not logically equivalent.

The universal quantifier $\forall$, in L_1, combines with a common noun K, a variable x, and a formula A to yield a formula $(\forall K,x)A$ (Definition 1(vi)). There is another way of introducing the universal quantifier which might appeal to some logicians (for example, Lewis Carroll). The quantifier $\wedge$ can be treated as combining with two common nouns to yield a formula. If K_1 and K_2 are common nouns, then $(\wedge K_1,K_2)$ is a formula. This new theory treats the form

All K_1's are K_2's

as basic, and sentences such as

All men are mortal

would be paraphrased as

All men are mortal men

for translation into the formal language. Given restricted common nouns, this new way of introducing the quantifier is equivalent to our old way. This is so in view of the equivalence of

$(\forall K,x)A$

and

$(\wedge K,(K,x)A)$.

Descriptions in L_1 are constructed from common nouns. If K is a common noun, then $\text{ꞁ}K$ is a term (Definition 1(viii)). Thus in L_1, the English expression

The man who likes Margaret

is represented as

$\text{ꞁ}(M,x)Lxm$ (cf. (2)).

An alternative way, which is closer to the standard treatment, is to take the description operator ι as combining with a common noun K, a variable x, and a formula A to yield the term $(\iota K,x)A$. This alternative has the virtue that descriptions can be obtained without restriction.

But the present treatment, it seems to me, is more natural and is closer to English—especially for phrases such as 'the man'.

Common nouns, it will be observed, never occur in predicative positions in L_1. Unlike predicates, they do not combine with singular terms to yield formulas. A sentence of English such as

(25) John is a man

is not represented in L_1 as a subject–predicate sentence. Rather, it is represented by

(26) $(\exists M,x)x=j$,

where M is understood as standing for the common noun 'man' and j for the name 'John'. The translation of (25) in L_1 takes seriously the occurrence of the determiner 'a' in it. And the 'is' in (25) is treated as an occurrence of the 'is' of identity, not of predication. A more perspicuous rendering of (25) would be

(27) John *is identical to* a man.

I do not wish to argue that (26) is *the* proper way of representing the logical form of (25). Such a claim, if it can be made, can be justified only in the context of a grammar of English. All I wish to urge is that (27) is synonymous with (25), and, therefore, (25) can be represented in L_1 by (26).

It is useful to introduce metalinguistic abbreviations for (26) and formulas like it.

Definition 3

(i) $K(t) = \mathrm{Df}\,(\exists K,x)x = t$.

(ii) $K[t] = \mathrm{Df}\,(\exists K,x)\Box\, x = t$, where x is the first variable not to occur in t or K.

The formula $K(t)$ can be read as saying that t is a K. How should we read $K[t]$? Unfortunately, there is no convenient English expression that says exactly what $K[t]$ says. I suggest we read it as saying

(28) Some K is necessarily identical to t.

This statement should be carefully distinguished from three different claims that are liable to be confused with it:

(29) It is necessary that t is a K,

(30) t is necessarily a K,

(31) t and a K are necessarily identical.

In (30) and (31) t occupies a nearly transparent position,[9] whereas in

9. Reasons for the qualification "nearly" are given on pages 88–89.

(28) and (29) it is fully opaque. Let *t* stand for the phrase 'the man in the corner'. Then (30) and (31) are about the actual man in the corner: (30) says roughly that in each possible world that man is a *K*, whereas (31) says that there is a *K* with whom this man is necessarily identical. To appreciate the difference, let *K* stand for 'man chewing gum', and suppose that the man in the corner is, as a matter of fact, chewing gum. Now (30) says of the man in the corner that gum chewing is among his essential properties—in each world that man would be found chewing gum. Statement (31), on the other hand, says of the man in the corner that he is necessarily identical to a man who is in fact chewing gum. Given our assumptions, (31) is true and (30) is false. I now explain the difference between (28) and (29): (29) says that the proposition *t* is a *K* is necessarily true—in each world w, *t* of w is a *K* in w; (28), on the other hand, says that *t* is identical to a *K* in the actual world, and in each world w, *t* in w is identical to that *K* in w. Let *t* be as before and let *K* stand for 'man in the corner'. Then (29) says that the proposition that the man in the corner is a man in the corner is necessarily true, whereas (28) says that there is a man in the corner and that man is identical to the man in the corner in each world. Proposition (28) presumably is false and (29) true.

Constructions (28)–(31) are admittedly made up. The meaning I have assigned them is not one with which they are naturally endowed. I am not concerned with *how* the distinctions I have drawn above are marked; I care only that they *are* marked.

All the common nouns of L_1 are, so to speak, one-place. Is this an unhappy limitation of L_1? Are there *relative* common nouns? Expressions can be found in natural languages which seem to be relative nouns, e.g., 'son'. This word, for instance, seems to be relational—relating sons to parents. I will not enter into a full discussion of relative nouns, but I note, first, that the systems developed here can readily be extended to encompass relative nouns, if there are any. Second, such expressions can also be accommodated in a logic extended to include adjectives—expressions that form common nouns out of common nouns. If L_1 is to be adequate for the semantics of natural languages, it is clear that it will need to be extended along these lines. There are adjectives, such as 'fake', which resist all reduction to other logical categories. Attributive adjectives (e.g., 'big') may be another example of adjectives that resist reduction (for more on these, see p. 85). In any case, it is clear that a separate category of adjectives is needed quite independently of the issue of relative nouns. Now, with adjectives available, we need not think of 'of Jones' in 'son of Jones' as filling one place of a two-place noun; rather we can think of it as an adjective modifying the ordinary one-place common noun 'son'.[10]

I close this section with a few observations on the quantifier $\exists$, misleadingly called the "existential" quantifier. Formulas in L_1 containing $\exists$, such as

(32) $(\exists K,x)Fx$,

can be straightforwardly read as

(33) Some *K* is *F*,

or even as

(34) There is a *K* that is *F*.

But the temptation to read (32) as

(35) There *exists* a *K* that is *F*

should be resisted. I do not know who is responsible for perpetrating the myth that (33) and (35) are equivalent, but it is this myth that gives plausibility to the dogma "to be is to be the value of a bound variable." Reject the myth and you reject the dogma. The nonequivalence of (33) and (35) is readily seen in an example. Sentence (36) surely is true:

(36) Some possible object does not exist.

But (37) is at best false:

(37) There exists a possible object that does not exist.

Statements (33) and (35) are equivalent for some readings of *K* and not for others.

This topic requires a more extensive treatment than I can offer here. The point to be noted at present is that existence statements are not generally represented in L_1 via the quantifier $\exists$. A proper translation of these requires an existence predicate. So existence is a *predicate*, but this is not to say that it is an attribute of objects.

10. Thomason has shown me that this maneuver does not always work. Common nouns 'successor of 2' and 'predecessor of 2', for instance, cannot be understood as resulting from adjectival modification of the one-place common nouns 'successor' and 'predecessor', respectively. In the domain of integers, the latter two common nouns have the same intension, but not the first two. In a logic with adjectives, but no relative nouns, these common nouns and others like them will have to be left unanalyzed.

PART II

The Semantics of L_1

§3. *Introduction*

Associated with each categorematic expression of any language are three entities of especial semantic significance: the expression's extension, its intension, and its sense or meaning. An expression's extension determines its (language-world) relation to the actual world; its intension determines its relation to all possible worlds; the sense determines its content for the user of the language. The very nature of language dictates that its categorematic expressions have all three of these entities associated with them.

Among the syncategorematic expressions are the logical operators and connectives. In general, a logical operator O combines with some n expressions $\alpha_1, \ldots, \alpha_n$ of categories $c_1, \ldots, c_n$ to yield an expression $O(\alpha_1, \ldots, \alpha_n)$ of category c_{n+1}. Moreover, and this is important, O performs a *systematic* operation on the semantic values of categories $c_1, \ldots, c_n$ to yield a semantic value of category c_{n+1}. A logical operator can be classified as *extensional*, *intensional*, or *hyperintensional*[11] according to whether the semantic value it transforms is the extension of the input expressions, their intension, or their sense. More accurately, an operator O is extensional if the extension of $O(\alpha_1, \ldots, \alpha_n)$ is a function of the extensions of $\alpha_1, \ldots, \alpha_n$; O is intensional if O is not extensional and the intension of $O(\alpha_1, \ldots, \alpha_n)$ is a function of the intensions of $\alpha_1, \ldots, \alpha_n$; O is hyperintensional if O is neither extensional nor intensional and the sense of $O(\alpha_1, \ldots, \alpha_n)$ is a function of the senses of $\alpha_1, \ldots, \alpha_n$. On the definitions given, the sentential connective 'and' is an extensional operator and 'It is necessary that' is an intensional operator. (An extensional operator such as 'and' also transforms in a systematic way the intension and the sense of input expressions to yield the intension and the sense of the output expression. But these transformations are fixed by the way it transforms the *extensions* of the input expressions.)

A logic of operators $O_1, \ldots, O_m$ displays their transformational properties, and on the basis of these properties it explains the logical

11. I borrow this term from Cresswell (1975).

features, such as validity, of various linguistic forms containing these operators. Fortunately, the transformational properties of the logical operators can be exhibited without dealing with the extensions, intensions, and senses, as such. Their representations suffice. The form of the semantics of an intensional logical operator, for example, is this: if $i_1, \ldots, i_n$ are the *representations* of the intensions of the input expressions, then the intension of the output expression is represented by $\mathbf{O}(i_1, \ldots, i_n)$. For the purposes of logic we may identify intensions with their representations.

The logic we are developing here has, besides the various extensional connectives, the intensional connective $\Box$. It has no hyperintensional operators. Hence our concern with the intensions of expressions. The semantics of L_1 will specify rules that compute the intension of a compound expression in terms of the intensions of its components. I give semantic rules of L_1 in §7 in the form of a definition of truth. First, I develop a theory of intensions for terms, predicates, sentences, and common nouns.

§*4. Terms, Predicates, and Sentences*

I follow the standard theory of the intensions of terms, predicates, and sentences. The intension of a term determines its referent in each possible world; the intension of a predicate determines what objects it is true of in each possible world; and the intension of sentence determines whether it is true or false in each possible world. (I suggest some modifications to this standard and familiar picture in chapter 3.) To obtain representations of these intensions, we need a representation of possible worlds and objects in them. This is done by a *model structure*.

Definition 4. A *model structure* for L_1 is an ordered triple $\langle W, D, i^* \rangle$, where

(i) W is a nonempty set,
(ii) D is a function that assigns to each member of W a nonempty set,
(iii) i^* is a function that assigns to each member w of W a member of D(w).

I think of W as representing a set of possible worlds and of D(w) as representing the set of objects that exist in w.[12] (Sometimes I shall give

12. Henceforth I shall often identify worlds with their representations. Thus I shall call $w \in W$ a world, and D(w) the set of objects existing in w.

the model structure a temporal interpretation. W, in this interpretation, represents moments of time, and D(w) represents the objects that exist at time w. Correspondingly, the object language connective $\Box$ is read "It is always the case that....") The third member of the model structure, i*, is a function of convenience. The value of i* in w is used to represent nonexistence in w. Thus if the uniqueness condition of a description is not met in w (if the description fails to denote in w), we make i*(w) the value of that description in w. Given this understanding of i*(w), it may seem objectionable to have i*(w) belonging to D(w).[13] But the force of the objection is reduced if we let i*(w) be one of the least interesting and the least talked about objects of w! D(w) is required to be nonempty primarily for convenience, but there is something to be said for the idea that a world with no objects in it is impossible.

Given a model structure $\mathfrak{A}\,(=\langle W,D,i^*\rangle)$ we can represent the intension of a term by a function that assigns to each world w, a member of D(w). Following Carnap, I call the intension of a singular term an *individual concept*.

Let $\mathfrak{A} = \langle W,D,i^*\rangle$ and $U = \bigcup_{w\in W} D(w)$.

Definition 5. An *individual concept* in $\mathfrak{A}$ is a function i from W into U such that $i(w)\in D(w)$ at all worlds w.

Example. i* is an individual concept in $\mathfrak{A}$.

Similarly, the intension of an *n*-place predicate, called from now on *n-ary relation*, can be represented by a function that assigns to each world w a set of *n*-tuples. If an *n*-tuple $\langle d_1,\ldots,d_n\rangle$ belongs to the representation of a predicate at a world w, then $d_1,\ldots,d_n$ stand in w in the relation expressed by the predicate.

Definition 6. An *n-ary relation* $(n>0)$ in $\mathfrak{A}$ is a function P from W into $\mathscr{P}(\underbrace{U\times\ldots\times U}_{n-\text{times}})$ such that if $\langle d_1,\ldots,d_n\rangle\in P(w)$, then $d_1,\ldots,d_n\in D(w)$.[14] A 1-ary relation is also called a *property*.

The intension of a sentence, a *proposition*, is represented by a set of

13. An alternative would be to require i* to be an object (not a function) which does not belong to $\bigcup_{w\in W} D(w)$. This fits better with the intuitive motivation for i*, but it is also inconvenient in various ways. For example, now $\sim F(\text{ɿ}(K,x)x \neq x)$ is logically valid if, as is plausible, the extension of a predicate at a world w is always included in D(w). This has undesirable consequences for the calculus of L_1.

14. We identify the 1-tuple $\langle d\rangle$ with d itself.

possible worlds. If w belongs to the representation of a sentence, then the sentence is true in w.

Definition 7. A *proposition* in $\mathfrak{A}$ is any subset of W.

The extension, and also the denotation, of a term in a world w is the value of its individual concept in w. Similarly, the extension of a predicate in w is the value of its intension at w. The extension of a sentence in w is The True if w is a member of its intension; otherwise, its extension is The False.

It is a consequence of my definitions that a name always denotes an existent object and that only existent objects bear relations expressed by predicates. These are objectionable consequences. We can have names for merely possible objects, and possible objects bear interesting relations to actual objects which can be expressed by predicates.[15] Our definitions could easily enough be altered to avoid these consequences, but I stick with them for simplicity.

§5. *Common Nouns*

Common nouns, like one-place predicates, are true or false of objects. The common noun 'animal', for example, is true of all and only animals, just as the predicate 'is circular' is true of all and only circular things. This similarity between common nouns and predicates has led semanticists and logicians to treat them alike. On the standard view, the extension of a common noun is represented by a set of objects, and its intension is represented by a property. In this section, I argue against the standard view and propose an alternative theory to replace it.

I remarked in §2 that common nouns and predicates behave differently in natural languages. Do these differences point to some semantic difference between them? Several philosophers have argued that they

15. For example, following Gibbard (1975), let a *piece* of clay be clay whose parts are stuck to each other. A piece of clay comes into existence when all its parts come to be stuck to each other and unstuck from all other clay. It perishes when some unstuck parts become stuck to it or some originally stuck parts become unstuck. Now let a and b be two distinct pieces of clay which in the actual world never become stuck to each other to form a larger piece of clay. Clearly, we can name the piece of clay that *would* result if a and b were to get stuck to each other. Let us call this possible piece of clay c. 'c' denotes a merely possible object. Further, c can bear relations to actual objects. c and a, respectively, bear the relation "heavier than"; Jones may bear the relation "thinks of" to c; and so on.

do. Geach has noted that only for some general terms *F* does the expression 'the same *F*' make sense. Geach divides general terms into "adjectival" and "substantival." A general term *F* is substantival for Geach if the expression 'the same *F*' makes sense. Dummett similarly distinguishes between two classes of general terms. (He attributes the distinction to Wittgenstein.) He says,

> In order to grasp the sense of a general term ['man', 'river', 'city'...,] we have to know, not only what is the criterion of its application, that is, when it is right to say of something that it is a man, a river, a city, but also the criterion of identity associated with it, that is, the correct use of '... is the same man as....'. (Dummett (1973) p. 546)

A little later Dummett says that general terms such as 'man' have as a part of their sense a criterion of identity but that the whole sense of terms such as 'red' resides in their criterion of application. Thus, for Dummett, the sense of general terms such as 'man' consists of both a criterion of identity and a criterion of application, and the sense of terms such as 'red' consists only of a criterion of application. Following Geach, he calls terms of the first sort "substantival" and terms of the second sort "adjectival." This distinction corresponds roughly to the distinction between common nouns and one-place predicates.

Geach and Dummett's observations are correct and important. They point to a semantic difference between common nouns and predicates. They show that there is a difference in their *senses*. However, it still needs to be shown that there are relevant differences in the *intensions* of common nouns and predicates. A further argument is required to show that the difference in sense indicates a difference in intension. Can such an argument be given?

Dummett seems to think that the difference between the two classes of terms is reflected *only* in sentences of a very simple sort—primitive sentences containing demonstratives—and that it is not relevant to sentences not containing them. Thus Dummett believes (if I understand him) that the difference in sense does not point to a difference in intension. First, he observes that successful employment of demonstratives does not require that they pick out an object. One may use the sentence 'that is red' properly and effectively though one is not predicating "red" of a particular object. He then goes on to say,

> Such adjectival terms [e.g., 'red', 'smooth'] quite naturally come to be used to make predications about objects... but it is not in view of their use to make predications about objects that we say of them that they have a criterion of application but no criterion of identity, but because they are used in a more primitive form of sentence 'That is Y' without occurring in statements of identification of the form 'This is the same Y (thing) as that'. (Dummett (1973) p. 573)

Dummett, it seems, holds that the semantic differences between common nouns and predicates appear only in the primitive discourse in which objects have not been articulated (in which "the amorphous lump of reality has not been carved into objects"). But once the domain of objects is fixed, no relevant semantic difference between common nouns and predicates remains. So Dummett appears to maintain that the difference in sense does not point to a difference in intension.

The standard theory is consistent with Geach and Dummett's observations. It is possible to maintain consistently that the semantic differences between common nouns and predicates occur only at the level of senses; that they are not reflected at the level of intensions and extensions. It can be argued that both "criterion of application" and "criterion of identity" are epistemic notions. The former gives the marks by which we recognize that an object falls under a common noun *K* (or a predicate *F*), and the latter gives us the marks by which we recognize the same *K* again. The metaphysical notion that corresponds to the criterion of application is the principle of application. The principle of application determines what objects the common noun is "true of." The metaphysical counterpart of criterion of identity is the principle of identity. But here it may be said that although there is content in the epistemic notion of the criterion of identity, the principle of identity is vacuous. When we are confronted with the same *K* on two occasions, we are confronted with the very same object: metaphysically, the criterion of identity is reflected in the self-identity of an object.[16]

16. I do not wish to suggest that Geach or Dummett hold anything like the theory I have sketched here. In particular, neither of them thinks that the principle of identity is trivial in the way indicated above.

Now we see a crucial presupposition of the standard view. It presupposes that the criterion of identity for any common noun helps us recognize the same object. But how can this supposition be justified? Why not allow the possibility that the same *K* may be two different metaphysical entities in different worlds (and different times) and that the principle of identity, instead of being vacuous, ties together those entities that are the same *K*?

I think that there are several reasons against supposing that the principles of identity are invariably trivial and vacuous. First, there are common nouns in English whose principles of identity are clearly nontrivial. Examples of such common nouns are 'passenger' and 'student'. The nontrivial character of the principle of identity of 'passenger' (in one sense of this common noun) is readily shown by the following paralogism. National Airlines served at least two million passengers in 1975. Every passenger is a person. *Ergo*, National Airlines served at least two million persons in 1975. A natural explanation of the invalidity of this argument is that although every passenger is a person, the principle of counting passengers is different from the principle of counting persons. That is, the principle of identity for 'passenger' is different from the principle of identity for 'person'. The person who boarded flight NA583 on 5 August 1975 is a different passenger from the person who boarded flight NA376 on 11 November 1975, but the two passengers are the same person. The principles of identity for 'passenger' and 'person' differ. The principle of identity for 'person' may be trivial; the principle of identity for 'passenger' is clearly nontrivial.

Another way of explaining the paralogism brings out the second reason against supposing that the principles of identity are invariably vacuous. It can be argued that the alleged paralogism is no paralogism at all but a perfectly valid argument. The false conclusion is to be explained by the fact that one of the premises, namely, that every passenger is a person, is false. Strictly speaking, the proponent of this view will say that a passenger is not a person. A passenger and a person are completely different kinds of objects. The two bear an intimate relation, but they are distinct objects nonetheless. Hence, in the sense in which fewer than two million *persons* traveled on National Airlines in 1975, a person and a passenger are distinct objects. It will be granted that there is a sense in which a passenger is a person, but in this reading of 'person' the proponent will argue that the conclusion of the argument is true. What I do not like about this view is its bloated ontology, its overcrowded planes, and its making simple things such as students and passengers overly mysterious. I would rather see passengers as persons but with a different principle of identity. My reason for this, or rather my second reason, is ontological parsimony.

Few of us believe that there are in our universe passengers besides persons. Therefore the solution of the paralogism in terms of principles of identity is more appealing than its solution in terms of an overinflated ontology. Now the technique that has proved useful to dispense with these mysterious objects may also be useful for dispensing with more familiar objects such as ships, shoes, and statues. We need not, for example, see an ontological difference between a statue and the matter of which it is made but only a difference in the principle of identity. (Some objections to this way of viewing things rely on treating all predications as extensional. These objections can be answered. See chapter 3, §4.) So a third reason for supposing principles of identity to be nontrivial is that such a supposition provides us with a tool to carry out ontological reduction and simplification.

I distinguish three principles associated with common nouns:

(1) Principle of trans-world identity,

(2) Principle of persistence,

(3) Principle of application.

The principle of persistence for a common noun *K* traces a *K* through time. It determines when an object at a time t is the same *K* as an object at another time t′. The principle of persistence can be quite simple. But it can also be quite complex, as with the noun 'ship', if, as I am inclined to do, we identify a ship at a time t with the planks, and so on, that constitute it at that time. In this case the principle of persistence will determine when a collection of planks at a time t is the same ship as another collection at time t′.

The principle of trans-world identity for a common noun *K* traces a *K* through possible worlds. There are two ways of understanding this principle, one more general and the other more restricted. We can think of the principle of trans-world identity as determining when an object in a world w at a time t is the same *K* as an object in another world w′ and time t′ (t′ possibly the same as t). In this more general sense, the principle of trans-world identity subsumes the principle of persistence. The other way of construing the principle is this. It determines when an object in w at t is the same *K* as an object in a world w′ at the same time t. In this way of understanding the principle, it neither implies nor is implied by the principle of persistence. We need both the principles to trace an object through times and worlds. (Note that the two principles define completely the relation "d in w at t is the same *K* as d′ in w′ at t′." If there is a time t″ at which both the *K* in w (d) and the *K* in w′ (d′) exist, we apply the principle of trans-world identity directly. If there is not such a time t″, we consider a series of other worlds to obtain one in which these *K*'s do overlap.) The principles of persistence and trans-world identity together constitute the principle of identity. The principle of identity for a common noun *K* traces *K*'s through worlds and times.[17]

The principle of application determines what objects the common noun is true of at each world w and time t. It neither entails nor is entailed by the principle of identity. Two common nouns may share the same principle of identity but differ on principles of application. Or they may share a principle of application but differ on principles of identity. An example of the former is 'boy' and 'man'. The principles of identity for these are the same. But not every man is a boy, so the principles of application differ. An example of the latter is 'passenger' and 'person traveling in a vehicle'. The principles of application now are the same—exactly the same things qualify as passengers and as persons traveling in a vehicle; their principles of identity, as we saw above, differ.

Evidence for the independence of the principles of identity and application is also provided by the considerations of vagueness. If the two principles were dependent on one another, we would expect vagueness in one to infect the other. But this does not seem to be so. 'Boy' is vague in its principle of application, but its principle of identity

17. Principles of identity, as I understand them, are associated with count nouns *and also with mass nouns.* The principle of identity for a count noun *K* traces a *particular K* through times and worlds. The principle of identity for a mass noun *K* traces a *particular quantity* of *K* through times and worlds. (For an explanation of the notion of quantity, see Cartwright (1965), (1970).)

is not correspondingly vague. Similarly, 'car' is vague in its principle of identity, but this vagueness is not reflected in its principle of application.

I should stress that, as I understand it, a principle of identity for a common noun *K* simply traces *K*'s through worlds and times. It does nothing more and nothing less. Thus, as I understand the concepts of principles of identity and application, the two senses of the word 'book' do not provide an example where the principle of application is shared but the principle of identity is not shared. So what I mean by 'principle of identity' is not quite the same thing as what others mean by 'criterion of identity'. Dummett, for example, thinks that the two senses of the word 'book' do provide an example where common nouns share a criterion of application but differ on criteria of identity. The reason he thinks this is that the truth conditions of 'this is a book' with either sense of 'book' are the same, but the truth conditions of 'this is the same book as that' differ. Nonetheless, despite the fact that the two senses of 'this is a book' have the same truth conditions, it does not follow that the two senses of 'book' are true of the same objects, and hence it does not follow that they share a principle of application. In general, the identity of truth conditions of 'that is a ϕ' and 'that is a ψ' does not imply that ϕ and ψ have the same extensions: for a counterexample, let ϕ be 'rabbit' and let ψ be 'undetached rabbit part'. The same observation applies to Geach's example of "type-word" and "token-word." On my view, these two common nouns do not share a principle of application.

In standard modal logics, intensions of common nouns are represented by properties (Definition 6). The intension of a common noun assigns to each world w (and/or time) objects that fall under the common noun in w. We now see that this representation is incomplete. It represents only the principle of application. An adequate representation must include the principle of identity.

There is another way of looking at this. Standard modal logics, on this view, take account of the principle of identity for common nouns. But the principle of identity for each common noun is exceedingly simple: d in w is the same *K* as d′ in w′ iff d = d′ (ignoring time and the problem mentioned on p. 27). The principles of identity for all common nouns are the same. To be the same *K* is to be the very same entity.

The objection against the standard view is now that it builds ontological presuppositions into the logic of common nouns. As a consequence, it obscures differences between predicates and nouns; it generates metaphysical perplexities, making objects more mysterious than they need be; and finally, it cannot give an adequate account of certain uses of some common nouns (e.g., 'passenger').

We now wish to discover a way of representing the intensions of common nouns. We want a representation that will capture both the principle of application and the principle of identity. This is done by *intensional properties*. Let $\mathfrak{A}$ $(=\langle W, D, i^* \rangle)$ be a model structure.

Definition 8. An *intensional property in* $\mathfrak{A}$ is a function $\mathscr{I}$ from W into the power set of the set of individual concepts in $\mathfrak{A}$ (cf. Definition 5).

An intensional property assigns to each world a set of individual concepts. It can be used to represent the intension of a common noun in the following way.

Proposition 1. Suppose that $\mathscr{I}$ represents the intension of a common noun *K* and that the individual concept i belongs to $\mathscr{I}$ at the world w; that is, $i \in \mathscr{I}(w)$. Then i(w) is a *K* in w, and i(w′) in w′ is the same *K* as i(w) in w.

Intensional properties may assign different sets of individual concepts to different worlds. The individual concept i may belong to an intensional property $\mathscr{I}$ at a world w but not at w′. These intensional properties represent intensions of common nouns such as 'boy' and 'man born in Jerusalem'. For instance, the noun phrase 'man born in Jerusalem' may apply to i(w) in w, because i(w) *is* a man born in Jerusalem, but the same man in w′, i.e., i(w′), may not be born in Jerusalem in w′. So i will belong to the intension of 'man born in Jerusalem' at w but not at w′.

This also shows that our understanding of intensional properties, formulated in Proposition 1, must be revised. It is inaccurate to say that if i belongs to the intension of *K* at a world w, then i(w′) in w′ is the same *K* as i(w) in w. It is inaccurate because it suggests that i(w′) in w′ is a *K*. I hold, however, that underlying every common noun, there is another that fulfills the condition of *modal constancy*.

Definition 9. An intensional property $\mathscr{I}$ in $\mathfrak{A}$ is *modally constant* iff $\mathscr{I}(w) = \mathscr{I}(w')$ at all worlds $w, w' \in W$.

A common noun fulfills the condition of modal constancy if its intension is modally constant. Observe that Proposition 1 applies exactly to such common nouns. Let i belong at w to the intension of a common noun *K* which fulfills the condition of modal constancy. Now we may say for any w′ that i(w′) in w′ is the same *K* as i(w) in w. The problem mentioned above does not arise because by definition i will also belong to $\mathscr{I}$ at w′.

This suggests a way of dealing with common nouns that do not fulfill the condition of modal constancy. Let [*K*] be the common noun that underlies *K* and fulfills the condition. Now we understand intensional properties thus:

Proposition 2. If i belongs to the intension of *K* at w, then i(w) is a *K* in w and i(w′) in w′ is the same [*K*] as i(w) in w.

It is a consequence of our conception of the intensions of common nouns that they pick out necessary existents. If a common noun *K* applies to an object i(w) in w, then that *K* (or better [*K*]) exists in all the worlds. This is so because individual concepts are total functions. They are defined at all worlds. So at any world w′, i(w′) is defined and, by Proposition 2, in w′ it is the same [*K*] as i(w) in w. Thus every [*K*] exists in all worlds. This is an undesirable consequence. Most common nouns do not pick out necessary existents. However, I persist with the assumption that common nouns of L_1 satisfy this requirement. My reasons are twofold. First, it simplifies the exposition. The main ideas I am trying to present are most easily appreciated with this simplification. Considerations of existence complicate matters in ways not germane to the present enterprise. Second, the logics presented here are useful despite the restricted class of common nouns that are admissible. In any case a more general conception of common nouns is developed in chapter 3, and some of the ways in which this general conception can be accommodated in a logic of modality and quantifiers are also explored there.

Not all intensional properties are suitable candidates for the intensions of common nouns. They must at least be *separated*. (The concept of separation was first articulated by Bressan in *A General Interpreted Modal Calculus* (1972). I am indebted to Bressan for this concept and for his very illuminating discussion of common nouns. The concept of separation defined below is not quite Bressan's concept of "modal separation"[18]; the differences arise because, unlike Bressan, I am also concerned with compound common noun phrases such as 'man born in Jerusalem'.)

Definition 10. An intensional property $\mathscr{I}$ in $\mathfrak{A}$ is *separated* iff all individual concepts i,i′ that belong to $\mathscr{I}$ at any worlds w, w′ are such that if $i(w_1) = i'(w_1)$ at a world w_1, then $i = i'$.

To see that intensions of common nouns must meet this condition of separation, suppose, for reductio, that the intension of some common noun, say 'person', is not separated. Then, by definition, some individual concepts i,i′ belong to the intension of 'person' at some worlds and $i(w) = i'(w)$ (= d, say) at a world w, but $i \neq i'$. Since $i \neq i'$, the values of i and i′ differ at some world, say w_1. That is, $i(w_1) \neq i'(w_1)$. But this means (see Proposition 1) that d in w is the same person as $i(w_1)$ in w_1 and that d in w is also the same person as $i'(w_1)$ in w_1. Transitivity of identity yields that $i'(w_1)$ in w_1 is the same person as $i(w_1)$ in w_1. This contradicts the hypothesis that $i(w_1) \neq i'(w_1)$.

This argument, I should note, is *not* intended to prove that a person cannot be identical to two distinct persons in another world or at another time. Rather, the argument is designed to show that only certain types of intensional properties properly represent intensions of common nouns. It *relies* on our intuition that a person cannot possibly be identical to two distinct persons to show that the intension of 'person' is separated.[19]

18. An intensional property may be modally separated (in Bressan's sense) in one world but not in another. My concept of separation (Definition 10) is not similarly world relative. Note also that the concept of separation is not the same as "modal separation in every world." The former concept is stronger than the latter. (The concept of "modal separation in every world" is the same as "weak separation" defined in note 19 below.) The relationship between separation and modal separation is this. Let $\mathscr{I}$ be an intensional property, and let $\mathscr{I}^{\cup}$ be the intensional property such that at any world w, $\mathscr{I}^{\cup}(w) = \bigcup_{w' \in W} \mathscr{I}(w')$. Then $\mathscr{I}$ is separated if and only if $\mathscr{I}^{\cup}$ is modally separated in every (any) world.

19. A weaker requirement on intensional properties deserves mention.

Definition 10a. An intensional property $\mathscr{I}$ in $\mathfrak{A}$ *is separated in the world* w iff all the individual concepts i, i′ that belong to $\mathscr{I}$ at w are such that if $i(w_1) = i'(w_1)$ at a world w_1, then $i = i'$.

Definition 10b. An intensional property $\mathscr{I}$ in $\mathfrak{A}$ is *weakly separated* iff $\mathscr{I}$ is separated in every world.

I think that weak separation is too weak a requirement on the intensions of common nouns. However, it is of formal interest in the study of the logic of common nouns. (*Added subsequently*: Weak separation may be of greater philosophical interest than I originally thought; see chapter 4.)

I have argued so far that the intensions of common nouns are at least separated. Can a stronger requirement be imposed on these intensions? In particular, can we reasonably require them to be *strongly separated*?

Definition 11. An intensional property $\mathscr{I}$ in $\mathfrak{A}$ is *strongly separated* iff all individual concepts i, i′ that belong to $\mathscr{I}$ at some worlds are such that if $i(w) = i'(w')$ at any worlds w, w′, then $i = i'$.
One argument against this requirement is its ontological ramifications. Ontologies consistent with the weaker requirement of separation are inconsistent with strong separation. Let us illustrate this.

Consider an ontology of space–time points. In this picture the metaphysically basic entities in a world are space–time points, and the objects of ordinary experience and thought are constructs out of these basic entities. The natural number 2, for instance, may be identified with the set of sets containing exactly two space–time points. A man might be identified with the manifold of space–time points he occupies during his life. (The exact construction does not matter.) Now it can be shown that the requirement of strong separation is inconsistent with this ontology.

Consider the common noun ‘man’ again. In each world it will be true of some space–time manifolds, and for each of these manifolds it will provide a principle of identity. That is, it will associate with a manifold b in w those manifolds b′ in worlds w′ such that the man who occupies b in w is *the same man* as the man who occupies b′ in w′. Now suppose that in a world w_1 a man Fred is born in the Royal Victoria Hospital, Montreal. He spends all his life in Montreal and dies there. Suppose that the space–time region he occupies is c. Now consider another world, w_2, just like w_1 but one in which Fred’s mother has to journey to London before Fred’s birth. In w_2 Fred is born in Guy’s Hospital and spends the rest of his life in the British Isles. Call the space–time region he occupies in this world d. Clearly, the individual concept i_F (the Fred-concept) will belong to the intension of the common noun ‘man’:

i_F:	w_1	– – – – – – – – –	w_2
	c	– – – – – – – – –	d

Now imagine that in w_2 Jones’s mother occupies the very same bed in the Royal Victoria Hospital which Fred’s mother occupied in w_1.

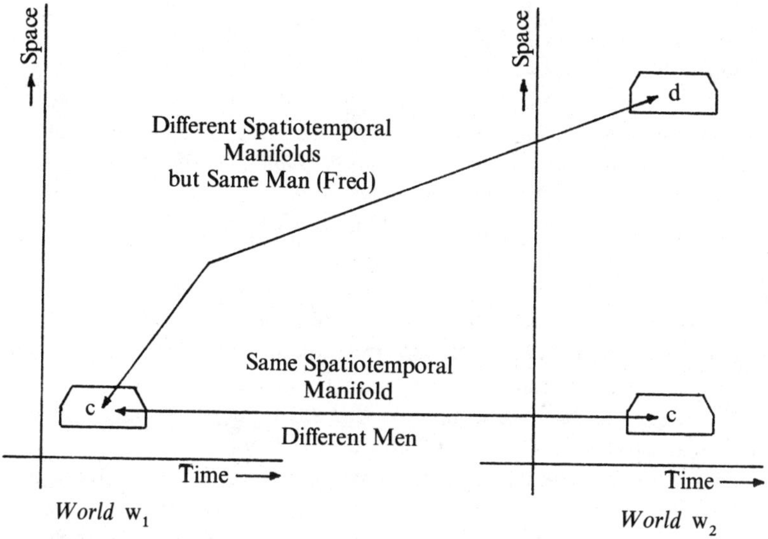

Figure 1

Imagine that Jones is born in w_2 in exactly the same place and at the same time as Fred is born in w_1 and that he spends his life in Montreal doing the same things at the same time as Fred does in w_1. Imagine, in summary, that Jones occupies the same space–time manifold in w_2 as Fred occupies in w_1. (See figure 1.) Such a situation is clearly conceivable. But now the Jones-concept i_J will also belong to the common noun 'man':

i_J:	w_1	— — — — — — — — —	w_2
	x	— — — — — — — — —	c

This is inconsistent with strong separation. Although i_J at w_2 agrees with i_F at w_1, i_J and i_F are distinct. Note that the requirement of separation will be met by the intension of the common noun 'man'. Two men cannot possibly occupy the same space–time manifold in the same world.

The requirement of strong separation, then, is inconsistent with the ontology of space–time points sketched above. And this I think is an argument against the requirement of strong separation. The argument here is *not* that the ontology under discussion is the right one, though it has been argued for by some physicists and philosophers. The argument is rather that the truth or falsity of this ontology is *not* a question of pure logic. It is a question that can be decided only by an investigation in physics and philosophy. Physics will decide if the fundamental laws of the universe are best expressed in an ontology of space–time points; and an investigation in philosophy will help us decide if the rest of our picture of the world can be accommodated within this ontology.

In case it is objected that it is not clear which questions are and which questions are not to be decided by pure logic, I should add that of two logical theories which otherwise are equally acceptable, we should choose the one that imposes fewer constraints on our ontology. Hence, unless there are positive arguments for strong separation, we should stick with the weaker requirement of separation.

Positive arguments for strong separation are hard to find. First, the formulas (and inferences) of L_1 validated by the stronger requirement are exactly those validated by the weaker requirement. So no arguments in favor of strong separation are to be found in the logical behavior of common nouns. Second, from the intuitive viewpoint, the requirement of strong separation occupies an uncomfortable middle ground between the weaker requirement and the traditional theory. Under the weaker requirement, the same man, for example, may be different space–time manifolds (or different collections of molecules or different hunks of reality) in different worlds. On the traditional view, however, the same man is the same *thing* (the same portion of the real) across worlds and across times. The same man cannot be a different metaphysical entity in another world; nor can the same entity be a different man in a different world. The weaker requirement rejects both these claims.

The requirement of strong separation, as I said, occupies a middle ground between the two. It allows the same man to be different entities in different worlds, but it disallows the same entity's being a different man in a different world. It disallows, that is, the situation described by (a)–(c):

(a) The individual d is a man in w,
(b) The individual d is a man in w′,
(c) The individual d in w is *not* the same man as d in w′.

But if we allow the same man to be different entities in different worlds, what intuitive motivation could there be for ruling out the situation described by (a)–(c)? I can see none.

The arguments against strong separation also justify our use of the five-place relation of identity:

$$d_1 \text{ in } w_1 \text{ is the same } K \text{ as } d_2 \text{ in } w_2.$$

Without further metaphysical assumptions, such as those of *Counterpart Theory*, any attempt to reduce the number of arguments in this relation is equivalent to putting stronger requirements on the intensions of common nouns. Strong separation, for instance, reduces the relation to a three-place one:

$$d_1 \text{ is the same } K \text{ as } d_2.$$

Our argument for preferring the five-place relation is that it yields a more general logic which accommodates all the logical inferences and is also ontologically neutral.

Let us call the intensions of common nouns *sorts*. Then the upshot of our discussion so far is that sorts are best represented by separated intensional properties. It is tedious, and for our purposes unnecessary, to distinguish between sorts and the functions that represent them. The distinction between the two should be understood, but once understood it need not be made (like the use–mention distinction). Sorts are sorts absolutely, not relative to this or that model structure. Functions, on the other hand, represent sorts (and can be treated as sorts) only relative to a model structure. The ontological character of separated intensional properties is quite clear—at least as clear as that of other mathematical objects. The ontological character of sorts is more mysterious and thus more debatable. Maybe sorts are mental entities; maybe they are dispositions of some very complex organisms; it may even be that they are constructs out of possible worlds. I do not know. And for our purposes it does not matter. We can display the logic of common nouns in terms of the representations of sorts. Sorts themselves are not needed.

Definition 12. A *sort* in a model structure $\mathfrak{A}$ is an intensional property in $\mathfrak{A}$ which is separated.

Henceforth we identify a sort with a function that represents it.

Variables '$\mathscr{S}$', '$\mathscr{S}'$', '$\mathscr{S}_1$', etc., are used to range over sorts (of a fixed model structure $\mathfrak{A}$).

An objection to our theory of the intensions of common nouns merits attention. It may be argued that there are common nouns in English whose intensions are not separated, e.g., 'thing Martha likes', 'physical object', 'red thing'. For instance, if both Fred and the space–time manifold c are things Martha likes, then both the Fred-concept and the space-time-manifold-c-concept will belong to the intension of 'thing Martha likes' at the actual world, thus violating the requirement of separation. Similarly, it can be argued that the intensions of 'physical object' and 'red thing' also violate the requirement of separation.

I should begin my reply by acknowledging that I do not have a completely satisfactory answer to this objection. The objection hinges on very general common nouns, 'thing' and 'object', and the logic of these expressions is almost as complicated as that of the copula 'be'. The simplest way out would be to say that such expressions as 'thing Martha likes', 'physical object', and 'red thing' do not belong to the *logical* category of common nouns. Syntactically and superficially, they behave like common nouns, but they are not really common nouns. This reply, however, would be convincing only if it were accompanied with an adequate theory of the perplexing nouns 'thing' and 'object'. A second way out is to say that these expressions are *incomplete* common nouns; that in 'thing Martha likes' the expression 'thing' is functioning like a variable whose substituends are common nouns. In this theory 'thing' and 'object' are *pro–common nouns*. They stand in place of common nouns proper, and sentences containing them express complete thoughts only when these "dummy" nouns are understood as meaning a proper sort or as bound to a quantifier. This theory gives a nice account of some sentences. For instance,

(38) Fred is a thing Martha likes

is understood as meaning

There is a sort $\mathscr{S}$ such that Fred is an $\mathscr{S}$ that Martha likes.

But there are various uses of "thing" expressions that are left unexplained. For instance,

(39) There are only two things that Martha likes

cannot be understood as meaning

There is a sort $\mathscr{S}$ such that there are only two $\mathscr{S}$ that Martha likes. It is hard to see what explanation the second theory would give of sentences like (39).

We can now see why lists of proper names do not belong to the category of common nouns. If a list such as 'one of John, Fred, and Mary' is treated as a common noun, then its intension presumably would have the John-concept, the Fred-concept, and the Mary-concept at each world. But now there is no guarantee that the condition of separation is fulfilled. It may well be that the John-concept and the Fred-concept, though distinct, coincide at some worlds.

My use of the term 'sort' is somewhat broader than its use in various philosophical works. As I use it, sorts need not give essential properties of objects. Common nouns such as 'man born in Jerusalem' express sorts, although "being a man born in Jerusalem" is not an essential property of any man. Sorts that give essential properties of objects I call *substance sorts.*

Definition 13. A *substance sort* in a model structure $\mathfrak{A}$ is a modally constant and separated intensional property.[20]

Substance sorts are sorts that are modally constant. 'Number', 'man', and 'river' express substance sorts,[21] but 'number of planets' and 'man born in Jerusalem' do not. Nouns that express substance sorts I call *substance nouns.* (These are nouns that fulfill the condition of modal constancy; see p. 28.) Some substance nouns express sorts that are *natural* (e.g., 'horse', 'water'); some express sorts that are *artificial* (e.g., 'number greater than three' and 'man identical to Jones'). Further, even a natural substance sort does not necessarily "pick out" the metaphysical subject of predication (e.g., 'river', 'statue'). I am inclined to think that a sort which picks out the metaphysical subject of predication will fulfill the condition of strong separation.

Given a sort $\mathscr{S}$ in $\mathfrak{A}$ we designate by $\mathscr{S}[w]$ the set of objects that fall under $\mathscr{S}$ in w.

Definition 14. $\mathscr{S}[w] = \text{Df } \{d : d \in D(w) \text{ and there is an individual concept } i \in \mathscr{S}(w) \text{ such that } i(w) = d\}$.

20. Substance sorts are called "absolute attributes" by Bressan.

21. This is not quite accurate. Strictly speaking, 'man', 'river' do not express substance sorts because they do not pick out necessary existents.

Definition 15. $\mathscr{S}[\![w]\!]$ = Df $\{d : d \in D(w)$ and there is an individual concept $i \in \mathscr{S}(w')$ for some $w' \in W$, such that $i(w) = d\}$.

$\mathscr{S}[\![w]\!]$ is the set of objects in w that are possibly $\mathscr{S}$.

Definition 16. d *in* w *is the same* $\mathscr{S}$ *as* d′ *in* w′ iff there is an individual concept i that belongs to $\mathscr{S}$ at some world and $i(w) = d$ and $i(w') = d'$.
Note that if d in w is the same $\mathscr{S}$ as d′ in w′, it does not follow that d (also, d′) is an $\mathscr{S}$ in w(w′). However, it does follow that d(d′) in w(w′) is possibly an $\mathscr{S}$, that is, $d \in \mathscr{S}[\![w]\!]$. Note also that the relation "is the same $\mathscr{S}$ as" is transitive in the sense that if d in w is the same $\mathscr{S}$ as d′ in w′ and d′ in w′ is the same $\mathscr{S}$ as d″ in w″, then d in w is the same $\mathscr{S}$ as d″ in w″. (This is a consequence of the separation of $\mathscr{S}$.) The relation is obviously symmetric. It is also weakly reflexive in the sense that if $d \in \mathscr{S}[\![w]\!]$, then d in w is the same $\mathscr{S}$ as d in w.

Suppose that the individual d is an $\mathscr{S}$ in w. Then there is a unique individual d′ which is that $\mathscr{S}$ in w′. Individual d′ can be said to be the $\mathscr{S}$ *counterpart* (manifestation) in w′ of d in w. Formally, the notion is defined thus:

Definition 17. The $\mathscr{S}$ *counterpart in* w′ *of the individual* d *in* w (abbreviated to $\mathscr{S}(w', d, w)$) is the unique individual d′ such that d′ in w′ is the same $\mathscr{S}$ as d in w.
Note that $\mathscr{S}(w', d, w)$ is well defined if $d \in \mathscr{S}[\![w]\!]$. For if $d \in \mathscr{S}[\![w]\!]$, then there is an individual concept i belonging to $\mathscr{S}$ at some world such that $i(w) = d$. Separation of $\mathscr{S}$ implies that i is unique. Hence there is a unique d′, namely i(w′), which in w′ is the same $\mathscr{S}$ as d in w.

The conclusions of this section and of the previous one are summed up in table 1.

Observe that the intensions of terms, *n*-place predicates, and sentences can be viewed as patterns of their extensions in various worlds. But the intensions of common nouns cannot be so viewed. Hence the semantics presented here is not "case-intensional," in Belnap's sense (see Belnap (1972) p. xv). If the extension of a common noun in a world is understood to be a set of individual concepts, then our semantics would be case-intensional; but this way of understanding the extension of a common noun does not fit with our intuitive idea of extension.

§6. *Models and Assignments*

We are now in a position to give the definition of a *model*.

Table 1

Expression	*Its Extension*	*Its Intension*	*Intension Represented by:*
1. Term	Object	Individual concept	A function that assigns to each world an object
2. *n*-Place predicate	A set of *n*-tuples of objects	*n*-ary relation	A function that assigns to each world a set of *n*-tuples of objects
3. Common noun	A set of objects	Sort	A function that assigns to each world a set of individual concepts (see (1)); the function is required to be separated
4. Sentence	A truth value	Proposition	A function that assigns to each world a truth value

Definition 18. A *model* for L_1 is an ordered quintuple $\langle W, D, i^*, m, \rho \rangle$, where

(i) $\langle W, D, i^* \rangle$ is a model structure for L_1,
(ii) m is a function that assigns (a) to each individual constant of L_1 an individual concept,[22] (b) to each *n*-ary predicate an *n*-ary relation, and (c) to each atomic common noun a sort,
(iii) $\rho \in W$.

A model for L_1 specifies the intension of each atomic expression (this is done by the function m) and the real world (ρ).[23] Semantic rules of L_1

22. Relativizations such as "for $\langle W, D, i^* \rangle$" will be omitted if the omission is unlikely to cause misunderstanding.

23. Models are sometimes thought of as representations of possible situations. This interpretation allows a strong parallel to be drawn between the logical notion of implication defined in terms of models and the intuitive notion of entailment defined in terms of possible situations. This way of thinking of models works pretty well if we confine ourselves to certain logics—e.g., first-order logics. (Actually, even here the idea encounters serious difficulties.) But with other logics, such as L_1, it is clearly inadequate. What

determine the intension of a complex expression in terms of the intensions of the atomic expressions that constitute it. We specify the semantic rules of L_1 in §7, in the form of a definition of truth.

Since the component expressions of a formula may contain free variables, the definition of truth proceeds via the definition of satisfaction. We define first the conditions under which a formula is satisfied by an *assignment* of values to the variables. The assignments for L_1, however, need to be a little more complicated than in standard logics; for variables in L_1 are bound to common nouns. And the common noun that binds a variable is relevant to determining the satisfaction conditions of subformulas such as $\Box Fx$. Thus variables of L_1 must be assigned, besides objects, common nouns that bind them (or their intensions). Assignments for L_1, then, assign to each variable an ordered pair. The first member of the ordered pair gives the sort that binds the variable, and the second member gives the object assigned to it.

Definition 19. An *assignment* for L_1 relative to a model M $(= \langle W, D, i^*, m, \rho \rangle)$ is a function that assigns to each variable of L_1 an ordered pair $\langle \mathscr{S}, d \rangle$, where $\mathscr{S}$ is a sort relative to the model structure $\langle W, D, i^* \rangle$ and $d \in U (= \bigcup_{w \in W} D(w))$.
If a is an assignment, then $a_o(x)$ is the object assigned to x by a and $a_s(x)$ is the sort assigned to x by a. We now define some concepts that will be of use later.

Definition 20. An assignment a (for L_1 relative to a model M) is *normal* in w iff $a_o(x) \in a_s(x)[\![w]\!]$ for all variables x.

Definition 21. An assignment a′ *is an* $\mathscr{S}$ *variant of* a *at* x *in* w iff

(i) a′ is just like a except perhaps at x (abbreviated to $a' \underset{x}{\simeq} a$),

possible situation could a model of L_1 be a representation of? The possible situation in which there are only such and such possibilities? Such possible situations seem incoherent.

Models of L_1 are best viewed this way. They are devices useful for exhibiting the logic of certain connectives and operators. Logical connectives transform the intensions or extensions or senses of expressions in systematic ways, and one aim of logic is to specify these transformations. This can be done without dealing with intensions, etc., as such; their representations suffice. Rules of logic have this form: if the intensions of expressions $\alpha_1, \ldots, \alpha_n$ are represented thus and so, then the intension of $O(\alpha_1, \ldots, \alpha_n)$ (where O is a logical operator) is represented by such and such. Models, so to speak, give us the antecedents of the rule. They specify the representations of the intensions of atomic expressions.

(ii) $a'_s(x) = \mathscr{S}$,
(iii) $a'_o(x) \in \mathscr{S}[w]$.

Definition 22. *The* w′ *variant of* a *relative to* w (abbreviated to f(w′,a,w)) is the unique assignment a′ that meets the following conditions:

(i) $a'_s(x) = a_s(x)$ at all variables x,
(ii) $a'_o(x)$ in w′ is the same $a_s(x)$ as $a_o(x)$ in w, at all variables x.

If these conditions are not met by any assignment, then f(w′,a,w) is undefined.

Intuitively, f(w′,a,w) assigns to each variable that unique object in w′ which is the same $\mathscr{S}$ as the object assigned to it by a in w. ($\mathscr{S}$ is the sort assigned to the variable by a and also by f(w′,a,w). The assignments a and f(w′,a,w) assign the same sorts to the same variables.) Consider an example. Suppose that our model has just three worlds, say w_1, w_2, and w_3. Suppose, for simplicity, that the assignment a assigns to each variable the same sort $\mathscr{S}$ and the same object d:

$\mathscr{S}$:	w_1	w_2	w_3
	dbc	dbc	cdd
	bcb		

In this diagram, 'dbc' stands for the individual concept whose value in w_1 is d, in w_2 is b, and in w_3 is c. Clearly, the intensional property $\mathscr{S}$ is separated and, therefore, it is a sort. What is $f(w_2,a,w_1)$? First, it assigns the sort $\mathscr{S}$ to all the variables. Next, to determine the object $f(w_2,a,w_1)$ assigns to a variable x, we determine which object in w_2 is the same $\mathscr{S}$ as d in w_1. This is done by picking out the unique individual concept belonging to $\mathscr{S}$ whose value in w_1 is d—in this example it is dbc—and taking its value in w_2, i.e., b. So

$f(w_2,a,w_1)$ assigns to each variable x, b.

Similarly,

$f(w_3,a,w_1)$ assigns c to x,
$f(w_2,f(w_3,a,w_1),w_3)$ assigns b to x.

Note that

$f(w_1,a,w_2)$ assigns c to x.

Hence $f(w_1,a,w_2)$ is not in general identical to $f(w_2,a,w_1)$.

The following facts concerning f and other concepts are easily verified.

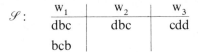

Facts

(1) Let a be normal in w. Then:

(i) f(w′,a,w) is well defined and is itself normal in w′ (though it need not be normal in w),

(ii) f(w,a,w) = a,

(iii) f(w″,a,w) = f(w″,f(w′,a,w),w′).

(2) If f(w′,a,w) is defined, then a is normal in w.

(3) If a is normal in w, then every $\mathscr{S}$ variant of a at any variable in w is normal in w.

§7. *Definition of Truth*

Let $M = \langle W, D, i^*, m, \rho \rangle$ be a model for L_1. Let $w \in W$ and let a be an assignment for L_1, relative to M, which is normal in w. We define by induction on the length of expression α, the following concept: *the semantic value of* α *at a world* w *in a model* M *relative to the assignment* a *normal in* w. We abbreviate this to $V^w_{M,a}(\alpha)$. First, it is useful to define the concept $I^w_{M,a}(\alpha)$ in terms of the valuation function V.

Definition 23. Let M, w, a, α be as above. Then $I^w_{M,a}(\alpha)$ is a function with domain W that satisfies the following condition:

$$(I^w_{M,a}(\alpha))(w') = V^{w'}_{M,f(w',a,w)}(\alpha).$$

Intuitively, $I^w_{M,a}(\alpha)$ gives the *intension* of an expression α in a model M, assignment a, and *world* w. Note that the intension of an expression is world relative. We now give the definition of the valuation function V.

Definition 24. Let M, w, a, α be as above.

V is defined by induction on α thus:

(i) If α is an individual constant, then
$V^w_{M,a}(\alpha) = m(\alpha)(w)$.

(ii) If α is a variable, then $V^w_{M,a}(\alpha) = a_o(\alpha)$.

(iii) If α is an atomic common noun, then
$V^w_{M,a}(\alpha) = m(\alpha)(w)$.

(iv) If α is the atomic formula $t_1 = t_2$, then
$V^w_{M,a}(\alpha) = T$ if $V^w_{M,a}(t_1) = V^w_{M,a}(t_2)$.
Otherwise, $V^w_{M,a}(\alpha) = F$.

(v) If α is the atomic formula $F(t_1, \ldots, t_n)$,
then $V^w_{M,a}(\alpha) = T$ if $\langle V^w_{M,a}(t_1), \ldots, V^w_{M,a}(t_n) \rangle \in m(F)(w)$.
Otherwise, $V^w_{M,a}(\alpha) = F$.

(vi) If α is the formula $\sim A$, then $V^{w}_{M,a}(\alpha) = T$ if $V^{w}_{M,a}(A) = F$. Otherwise, $V^{w}_{M,a}(\alpha) = F$.

(vii) If α is the formula $(A \supset B)$, then $V^{w}_{M,a}(\alpha) = T$ if $V^{w}_{M,a}(A) = F$ or $V^{w}_{M,a}(B) = T$. Otherwise, $V^{w}_{M,a}(\alpha) = F$.

(viii) If α is the formula $\Box$ A, then $V^{w}_{M,a}(\alpha) = T$ if $V^{w'}_{M,f(w',a,w)}(A) = T$ at all worlds $w' \in W$. Otherwise, $V^{w}_{M,a}(\alpha) = F$.

(ix) If α is the formula $(\forall K,x)A$, then $V^{w}_{M,a}(\alpha) = T$ if $V^{w}_{M,a'}(A) = T$ for all assignments a′ that are $I^{w}_{M,a}(K)$ variants of a at x in w. Otherwise, $V^{w}_{M,a}(\alpha) = F$.

(x) If α is the common noun $(K,x)A$, then $V^{w}_{M,a}(\alpha)$ is the set of individual concepts i such that $i \in V^{w}_{M,a}(K)$ and $V^{w}_{M,a'}(A) = T$, where $a' \underset{x}{\simeq} a$ and $a'_s(x) = I^{w}_{M,a}(K)$ and $a'_o(x) = i(w)$.

(xi) If α is the term $\urcorner K$, then $V^{w}_{M,a}(\alpha)$ is the value of the individual concept i at w if i is the unique concept belonging to $V^{w}_{M,a}(K)$. Otherwise, $V^{w}_{M,a}(\alpha) = i^*(w)$.

We say that a formula *A is satisfied by the assignment* a *at a world* w *in a model* M (abbreviated to $M,a \overset{w}{\models} A$) iff $V^{w}_{M,a}(A) = T$. A formula *A is true at a world* w *in a model* M ($M \overset{w}{\models} A$) iff *A* is satisfied at w in M by all assignments normal in w. *A is true in a model* M ($M \models A$) iff *A* is true at ρ in M. And, finally, a set of formulas Γ is true at w in a model M iff all members of Γ are true at w in M.

Remarks on Definition 24.

1. Since the valuation function $V^{w}_{M,a}$ is supposed to be defined for all *and only* those assignments a which are normal in w, we need to verify that the recursive clauses do not implicitly refer to nonnormal assignments. Clauses (viii)–(x) need particular attention in this respect. The correctness of clause (viii) is guaranteed by Fact 1(i) of §6, which states that if a is normal in w, then f(w′,a,w) is normal in w′. Further, in view of Fact 3, clauses (ix) and (x) are correct if $I^{w}_{M,a}(K)$ is a sort. And $I^{w}_{M,a}(K)$ is easily shown to be a sort by mathematical induction. If *K* is an atomic common noun, then $I^{w}_{M,a}(K) = m(K)$ and hence is a sort by the definition of m. On the other hand, if *K* is a compound common noun $(K',x)A$, then by clause (x) $V^{w'}_{M,a'}(K) \subseteq V^{w'}_{M,a'}(K')$ at all w′ and a′. Hence

$[I^w_{M,a}(K)](w') \subseteq [I^w_{M,a}(K')](w')$, at all worlds w'. Since $I^w_{M,a}(K)$ is a sort, by hypothesis of induction we conclude that $I^w_{M,a}(K)$ is a sort, too.

2. Note that although the clauses of induction above use the function I, it is used only for shorter expressions. Hence the use of I in the above definition is legitimate. It could in fact be eliminated but at the cost of brevity.

3. Clause (viii) is perhaps the most distinctive of my semantics. To see its motivation, consider the conditions under which a person, d, may be said to be essentially rational. Intuitively, what we do is this. We see if d is rational in the actual world. And then we determine in each world w if the *same person* is rational in w. More formally, the person d satisfies the formula $\Box Rx$ (where R stands for the predicate 'is rational') if d satisfies Rx in the actual world and if in w, Rx is satisfied by e, where e in w is the same person as d in the actual world. This motivates why we shift the values of the variables when we shift to a different world. We shift the values to get an entity that is the same person as the one we started out with. More generally, if x is assigned the sort $\mathscr{S}$, then the new value of x is the same $\mathscr{S}$ as the old value, though it may not be the very same object, the very same metaphysical entity.

4. Here is a formal illustration of clause (viii). Let the assignment a be as specified on page 39. That is, a assigns to each variable the sort $\mathscr{S}$ and the object d. Let the predicate F be assigned the property P.

P:

w_1	w_2	w_3
b,d	b	c,d

Now by clause (viii), $\Box Fx$ is satisfied by a in w_1 iff

(i) Fx is satisfied by $f(w_1, a, w_1)$ in w_1,

(ii) Fx is satisfied by $f(w_2, a, w_1)$ in w_2,

(iii) Fx is satisfied by $f(w_3, a, w_1)$ in w_3.

Clearly, $f(w_1, a, w_1) = a$ (Fact 1(ii)). Hence $f(w_1, a, w_1)$ assigns to x, d. By a simple inspection of the property P we discover that (i) is true. Further, we saw that $f(w_2, a, w_1)$ assigns to x, b. Hence (ii) is true. Condition (iii) is also easily seen to be true: $f(w_3, a, w_1)$ assigns to x, c. We conclude by clause (viii) that, in the model constructed, $\Box Fx$ is satisfied by a in w_1. Similarly, it can be shown that $\Box Fx$ is *not* satisfied by a in w_3.

§8. *Logical Concepts*

We adopt the standard definitions of the various logical concepts. In particular, we say that a set of formulas Γ is *satisfiable* iff there is an assignment a which satisfies every member of Γ at a world w in a model M. A set of formulas Γ *logically implies* a formula A iff $\Gamma \cup \{\sim A\}$ is not satisfiable. A formula A is *valid* iff $\{\sim A\}$ is not satisfiable. A formula is *invalid* iff it is not valid. A schema is *valid* iff all its instances are valid; otherwise, we say that the schema is *invalid*.

§9. *Some Valid Formulas*

A detailed study of the valid and invalid formulas of L_1 is left for chapter 2, where I present a calculus for L_1. Here I draw attention to some formulas of philosophical interest.

Barcan schema

(40) $(\forall K,x)\Box A \supset \Box(\forall K,x)A$

is invalid in L_1. Let a model assign to K the sort $\mathscr{S}'$ and to the one-place predicate F the property P′ displayed below:

$\mathscr{S}'$:

w_1	w_2
aa	aa
	bb

P′:

w_1	w_2
a	a

Now the antecedent of the Barcan formula,

(41) $(\forall K,x)\Box Fx \supset \Box(\forall K,x)Fx$,

is true in the world w_1, but the consequent is false in w_1. The invalidity of (41) is in accord with intuition. Intuitively, formulas such as (41) do not express logical truths. For although it may be true that

Every animal on Joe's farm is essentially a pig,

for on Joe's farm there are only pigs, it does not follow that

It is necessary that every animal on Joe's farm is a pig.

Joe might also have grown chickens on his farm.

The converse Barcan schema (42) similarly fails:

(42) $\Box(\forall K,x)A \supset (\forall K,x)\Box A$.

A model that assigns to K the sort $\mathscr{S}''$ and to F the property P″ falsifies (43):

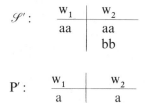

(43) $\Box(\forall K,x)Fx \supset (\forall K,x)\Box Fx$

$\mathscr{S}''$:

w_1	w_2
ab	ba

P'':

w_1	w_2
a	a

Counterexamples to the converse Barcan formula are easy to find. For instance, although

(44) It is necessary that every bachelor is unmarried

is true,

(45) Every bachelor is necessarily unmarried

is false.

Barcan formulas and converse Barcan formulas fail in L_1, and this fits well with our intuitions. However, both are valid in L_1 if the range of the common noun is restricted to substance nouns. Consider the Barcan formula (41) and suppose, for reductio, that it is not satisfied in w by an assignment a normal in w at a model M which assigns to K a substance sort. That is, we have

(46) $\text{M},\text{a} \overset{\text{w}}{\models} (\forall K,x)\Box Fx,$

(47) $\text{M},\text{a} \overset{\text{w}}{\not\models} \Box(\forall K,x)Fx.$

Formula (47) yields by Definition 24(viii) that there is a w′ such that

(48) $\text{M},\text{a}' \overset{\text{w}'}{\not\models} (\forall K,x)Fx$ where $\text{a}' = \text{f}(\text{w}',\text{a},\text{w})$.

Formula (48) implies (Definition 24(ix))

(49) $\text{M},\text{a}'' \overset{\text{w}'}{\not\models} Fx$ for some a″ such that a″ is an m(K) variant of a′ at x in w′.

Now consider the assignment a* constructed as follows. Let a* be just like a except perhaps at x (i.e., $\text{a}^* \underset{x}{\doteqdot} \text{a}$). Further, let a* assign to x the sort m(K) and the object that is the m(K) counterpart in w of $\text{a}''_0(x)$ in w′. That is, a* assigns to x the object $\text{m}(K)(\text{w},\text{a}''_0(x),\text{w}')$. (See Definition 17.) Now the definition of substance sort implies that a* is an m(K)-variant of a at x in w. Hence by (46) and Definition 24(ix) we conclude that $\text{M},\text{a}^* \overset{\text{w}}{\models} \Box Fx$. Therefore,

(50) $\text{M},\text{f}(\text{w}',\text{a}^*,\text{w}) \overset{\text{w}'}{\models} Fx$ (Definition 24(viii)).

But it is easily seen that $f(w',a^*,w) = a''$. So (50) implies

$M,a'' \models^{w'} Fx,$

contradicting (49).

We can express in L_1 the concept of a *substance sort*.

Definition 25. K is a *substance sort* = Df $\Box(\forall K,x)\Box K(x)$.

In L_1, then, formulas

(51) K is a substance sort $\supset .(\forall K,x)\Box A \supset \Box(\forall K,x)A$,

(52) K is a substance sort $\supset .\Box(\forall K,x)A \supset (\forall K,x)\Box A$

are valid. Intuitively, (51) and (52) do not express logical truths. The reason for the divergence between L_1 and our intuitions is that common nouns of L_1 pick out necessary existents, but nouns that are ordinarily regarded as substantival do not always pick out necessary existents. (In chapter 3, L_1 is improved on in this respect.) It can be seen that if K is restricted to common nouns that are substantival *and* that pick out necessary existents (e.g., 'number'), then the Barcan and the converse Barcan formulas express intuitive logical truths.

Similarly, schema

(53) $(\exists K,x)\Box A \supset \Box(\exists K,x)A$

does not hold for arbitrary K, but it does hold when K is understood to be a substance noun. Schema

(54) $\Box(\exists K,x)A \supset (\exists K,x)\Box A$

fails even when K is a substance noun.

Identity in L_1 is contingent if the two terms flanking the identity sign are closed. That is, the schema

$$s = t \supset \Box s = t \qquad (s \text{ and } t \text{ closed})$$

is not valid in L_1. If the terms flanking the identity sign are variables, then identity is contingent if the variables are bound to different common nouns; it is necessary otherwise. Schema (55) is not valid, but schema (56) is valid in L_1:

(55) $(\forall K,x)(\forall K',y)(x = y \supset \Box x = y)$,

(56) $(\forall K,x)(\forall K,y)(x = y \supset \Box x = y)$.

Finally, analyses (21) and (22) of (15) and (16), respectively, are vindicated in L_1 by the validity of

(57) $(\forall(K,x)A,x)B \equiv (\forall K,x)(A \supset B)$,

(58) $(\exists(K,x)A,x)B \equiv (\exists K,x)(A \wedge B)$.

§*10. Some Semantic Metatheorems*

We state without proof several useful metatheorems about the semantics of L_1. The proofs of these theorems are for the most part quite straightforward.

Let $M = \langle W, D, i^*, m, \rho \rangle$ be a model, $w \in W$, and let a be an assignment normal in w.

MT1. For all formulas A, $V^w_{M,a}(A) = T$ or $V^w_{M,a}(A) = F$.

MT2. Let α be any expression and let $x_{i_1}, \ldots, x_{i_n}$ contain all the variables that occur free in α. Further, let a, a′ be assignments normal in w, which agree on $x_{i_1}, \ldots, x_{i_n}$ (i.e., a, a′ assign the same values to $x_{i_1}, \ldots, x_{i_n}$). Then $V^w_{M.a}(\alpha) = V^w_{M,a'}(\alpha)$.

MT3. Let α be a closed expression. And let a, a′ be assignments normal in w. Then $V^w_{M,a}(\alpha) = V^w_{M,a'}(\alpha)$.

Let V^w_M be the function with the set of closed expressions of L_1 as its domain, satisfying the condition that $V^w_M(\alpha) = V^w_{M,a}(\alpha)$ at all assignments a normal in w. MT3 assures us that V^w_M is a well-defined function at all M and w.

MT4.

(i) $V^w_{M,a}(A \vee B) = T$ iff $V^w_{M,a}(A) = T$ or $V^w_{M,a}(B) = T$.

(ii) $V^w_{M,a}(A \wedge B) = T$ iff $V^w_{M,a}(A) = T$ and $V^w_{M,a}(B) = T$.

(iii) $V^w_{M,a}(A \equiv B) = T$ iff either $V^w_{M,a}(A) = T$ and $V^w_{M,a}(B) = T$ or $V^w_{M,a}(A) = F$ and $V^w_{M,a}(B) = F$.

(iv) $V^w_{M,a}(\Diamond A) = T$ iff there is a world $w' \in W$ such that $V^w_{M,f(w',a,w)}(A) = T$.

(v) $V^w_{M,a}((\exists K,x)A) = T$ iff there is an assignment a′ which is an $I^w_{M,a}(K)$ variant of a at x in w and which satisfies A at w in M.

(vi) $V^w_{M,a}((\exists! K,x)A) = T$ iff there is a unique assignment a′ which is $I^w_{M,a}(K)$ variant of a at x in w and it satisfies A at w in M.

(vii) $V^w_{M,a}(K(t)) = T$ iff there is an individual concept $i \in V^w_{M,a}(K)$ and $i(w) = V^w_{M,a}(t)$.

(viii) $V^w_{M,a}(K[t]) = T$ iff $I^w_{M,a}(t) \in V^w_{M,a}(K)$.

MT5. Let α be a closed expression. Then:

(i) If α is a constant, $V^w_M(\alpha) = m(\alpha)(w)$.

(ii) If α is a basic common noun, $V^w_M(\alpha) = m(\alpha)(w)$.

(iii) If α is the formula $t_1 = t_2$, $V^w_M(\alpha) = T$ iff $V^w_M(t_1) = V^w_M(t_2)$.

(iv) If α is the formula $F(t_1, \ldots, t_n)$, $V^w_M(\alpha) = T$ iff $\langle V^w_M(t_1), \ldots, V^w_M(t_n)\rangle \in m(F)(w)$.

(v) If α is the formula $\sim A$, $V^w_M(\alpha) = T$ iff $V^w_M(A) = F$.

(vi) If α is the formula $(A \supset B)$, $V^w_M(\alpha) = T$ iff either $V^w_M(A) = F$ or $V^w_M(B) = T$.

(vii) If α is the formula $\Box A$, $V^w_M(\alpha) = T$ iff $V^{w'}_M(A) = T$ at all w'.

(viii) If α is the formula $K[t]$, $V^w_M(\alpha) = T$ iff there is an individual concept $i \in V^w_M(K)$ such that $i(w') = V^{w'}_M(t)$ at all worlds w'.

(ix) If α is the term $\urcorner K$, $V^w_M(\alpha) = d$ iff either there is a unique individual concept $i \in V^w_M(K)$ and $i(w) = d$ or there is not a unique member of $V^w_M(K)$ and $d = i^*(w)$.

MT6. Suppose that t_1, t_2 are terms free for x in A and that no free occurrence of x in A falls within the scope of $\Box$. Now, if M is a model, w a world, and a an assignment normal in w, then $V^w_{M,a}(A^{t_1}/x) = V^w_{M,a}(A^{t_2}/x)$ if $V^w_{M,a}(t_1) = V^w_{M,a}(t_2)$.

MT7. Let A be a formula, x a variable, and t a term free for x in A. Let M be a model and a an assignment normal in w. Further, let the assignment $a' \underset{x}{\cong} a$ be such that $a'_s(x) = I^w_{M,a}(K)$ and $a'_o(x) = V^w_{M,a}(t)$. Then $V^w_{M,a}(A^t/x) = V^w_{M,a'}(A)$, provided $V^w_{M,a}(K[t]) = T$.

2 A Logical Calculus

In this chapter I present a calculus C_1, and I show that it is adequate for L_1 in the following sense. If a set of formulas Γ logically implies a formula A in L_1, then A is deducible from Γ in C_1. And conversely, if A is deducible from Γ in C_1, then Γ logically implies A.

§*1. The Calculus* C_1

All instances of the axiom schemata AS1–AS16 are axioms of C_1.

AS1. $A \supset (B \supset A)$.

AS2. $(A \supset (B \supset C)) \supset .(A \supset B) \supset (A \supset C)$.

AS3. $(\sim B \supset \sim A) \supset .(\sim B \supset A) \supset B$.

AS4. $\Box A \supset A$.

AS5. $\Box(A \supset B) \supset .\Box A \supset \Box B$.

AS6. $\sim \Box A \supset \Box \sim \Box A$.

AS7. $K[t] \supset .(\forall K,x)A \supset A^t/x$, provided t is free for x in A.

AS8. $(\forall K,x)(A \supset B) \supset .(\forall K,x)A \supset (\forall K,x)B$.

AS9. $A \supset (\forall K,x)A$, provided x is not free in A.

AS10. $(\forall K,x)K[x]$,[1] provided x is not free in K.

AS11. $t = t$.

AS12. $s = t \supset .A^s/x \supset A^t/x$,[2] provided s and t are free for x in A and no free occurrence of x in A is within the scope of a $\Box$.

AS13. $(\Diamond K[t_1] \wedge \Diamond K[t_2]) \supset .t_1 = t_2 \supset \Box t_1 = t_2$.

AS14. $(\exists! K,x)x = x \supset K(\urcorner K)$.

AS15. $\sim (\exists! K,x)x = x \supset \urcorner K = \urcorner(K',y)y \neq y$.

AS16. $(\forall(K,x)A,x)B \equiv (\forall K,x)(A \supset B)$.

Rule for Axioms. If A is an axiom, then $(\forall K,x)A$ and $\Box A$ are axioms also.

Rule of Inference. Modus Ponens. From A and $(A \supset B)$ infer B.

1. Whether AS10 is independent or not is an open question.
2. I am indebted to Belnap for this formulation of the principle of substitution of identicals.

The notions of "proof," "derivation," "theorem," and "deducibility" are given the usual definitions. We use '$\vdash A$' to abbreviate the claim that A is a theorem of C_1, and '$\Gamma \vdash A$' to abbreviate the claim that A is deducible from Γ in C_1. We say that a set of formulas Γ is *inconsistent* (in C_1) iff $\Gamma \vdash A$ and $\Gamma \vdash \sim A$, for some formula A.

Of the above axiom schemata, AS10, AS13, and AS16 are new and peculiar to the calculus C_1. These deserve special comment. AS10 says roughly that every K is such that some K is necessarily identical to it (see p. 14). This axiom schema clearly expresses an intuitive logical truth and is also valid in L_1. AS10 cannot be strengthened to

AS10′. $(\forall K,x)\Box K[x]$ (x not free in K).

AS10′ is not valid in L_1; it would be valid if all common nouns of L_1 fulfilled the condition of modal constancy. When a language has restricted common nouns, such a condition is usually inappropriate. AS13 ensures that all common nouns of L_1, simple or compound, are separated. An equivalent version of this axiom is

AS13′. $(\Diamond K[t_1] \wedge K[t_2]) \supset .\Diamond t_1 = t_2 \supset \Box t_1 = t_2.$

If AS13′ is weakened to

AS13″. $(K[t_1] \wedge K[t_2]) \supset .\Diamond t_1 = t_2 \supset \Box t_1 = t_2,$

then the axiom schema is satisfied as long as all common nouns are *weakly* separated. (See Definition 10b, chapter 1.) Finally, AS16 ensures that the Fregean equivalences are provable in C_1. That is, it ensures that a sentence such as

Every K that is F is G

is provably equivalent (in C_1) to

Every K is such that if it is F, it is G.

§2. *Some Syntactic Metatheorems*

Metatheorems 1–9 listed below indicate that the calculus C_1 is "well behaved." They are easily shown to hold for C_1 by standard techniques, so I omit their proofs. MT10 says essentially that a very weak version of the Barcan formula holds in C_1. And it is all we need to prove the crucial metatheorem MT11. MT12 lists for easy reference some theorems of C_1.

MT 1. If A is an instance of a tautology, then $\vdash A$. (Cited as PC.)
MT 2. If A is an instance of a theorem of S5, then $\vdash A$. (Cited as S5.)
MT 3. (Deduction theorem.) If $\Gamma, A \vdash B$, then $\Gamma \vdash (A \supset B)$.
MT 4. If $\Gamma \cup \{\sim A\}$ is inconsistent, then $\Gamma \vdash A$.
MT 5. If x is not free in Γ, then $\Gamma \vdash (\forall K, x)A$ if $\Gamma \vdash A$.
MT 6. If Γ is modally closed, then $\Gamma \vdash \Box A$ if $\Gamma \vdash A$.
MT 7. $\vdash (\forall K, x)A \equiv (\forall K, y)A'$, and
$\vdash (\exists K, x)A \equiv (\exists K, y)A'$,

where A differs from A' only in having x free where, and only where, A' has y free. (A and A' are said to be *alphabetic variants.*)

MT8. (Replacement theorem.) Let α be any expression. And let α' be the expression obtained by substituting A' for some occurrences of A in α. Then supposing $\vdash A \equiv A'$,

$\vdash \alpha \equiv \alpha'$, if α is a formula,
$\vdash \alpha = \alpha'$, if α is a term,
$\vdash \alpha[t] \equiv \alpha'[t]$, if α is a common noun.

MT9. If b does not occur in Γ or in A, then $\Gamma \vdash (\forall K, x)A$ if $\Gamma \vdash A^b/x$.

MT10. If $\vdash (\forall K, x)\Box(A \supset \Box B)$, then $\vdash A \supset \Box(\forall K, x)B$, provided x is not free in A.

Proof of MT 10

Suppose

(i) $\vdash (\forall K, x)\Box(A \supset \Box B)$.

Since

(ii) $\vdash \Box(C \supset D) \supset (\Diamond C \supset \Diamond D)$ (S5),

we get

(iii) $\vdash (\forall K, x)(\Diamond A \supset \Diamond \Box B)$ (AS8, MT5).

Also,

(iv) $\vdash \Diamond \Box B \supset B$ (S5);

hence

(v) $\vdash (\forall K, x)(\Diamond A \supset B)$ ((iii), (iv), MT5, AS8).

Therefore,

(vi) $\vdash \Diamond A \supset (\forall K, x)B$ (AS8, 9, (v)),

since x is not free in A.

By MT6,

(vii) $\vdash \Box(\Diamond A \supset (\forall K, x)B)$;

that is,

(viii) $\vdash \Box\Diamond A \supset \Box(\forall K,x)B$ (AS5).

But

(ix) $\vdash A \supset \Box\Diamond A$ (S5).

So

(x) $\vdash A \supset \Box(\forall K,x)B$ ((viii), (ix), PC).

MT10 says that the rule

$$\text{R}: \frac{(\forall K,x)\Box(A \supset \Box B)}{A \supset \Box(\forall K,x)B}$$

is *admissible* in C_1; that is, if the premise of R is *provable*, then the conclusion of R is also provable in C_1. Note that the rule is not *derivable* in C_1: if the premise of R is deducible from a set of formulas Γ, the conclusion is not necessarily deducible from Γ. If R were derivable in C_1, then the Barcan formula would be provable in C_1. For

(i) $\vdash \Box B \supset \Box(A \supset \Box B)$ (S5).

Hence

(ii) $(\forall K,x)\Box A \vdash (\forall K,x)\Box(T \supset \Box A)$ ((i), MT5, AS8),

where T is any instance of a tautology not containing x free. Now by the supposed derivability of R we get

$$(\forall K,x)\Box A \vdash T \supset \Box(\forall K,x)A.$$

Hence

$$(\forall K,x)\Box A \vdash \Box(\forall K,x)A$$

and

$$\vdash (\forall K,x)\Box A \supset \Box(\forall K,x)A \quad \text{(deduction theorem).}$$

So if R were derivable in C_1, C_1 would be unsound. The soundness of C_1, established in §3, shows that R is not derivable. Note that derivability of R is equivalent (in "normal" systems) to the validity of the Barcan formula.

MT11. If b does not occur in the theory Γ or in the formula A, then $\Gamma \vdash \Box(\forall K,x)A$ if $\Gamma \vdash \Box A^b/x$.

Proof of MT11. Suppose that b does not occur in Γ or in A and that $\Gamma \vdash \Box A^b/x$. Then there is a finite subset, say $\{B_1,\ldots,B_n\}$, of Γ such that

$$B_1,\ldots,B_n \vdash \Box A^b/x.$$

Hence by the deduction theorem,

$$B_1,\ldots,B_{n-1} \vdash B_n \supset A^b/x.$$

Applying the deduction theorem $n-1$ times, we get

$$\vdash (B_1 \supset (B_2 \supset \ldots (B_n \supset \Box A^b/x)\ldots)).$$

So

$$\vdash (B_1 \wedge B_2 \wedge \ldots \wedge B_n) \supset \Box A^b/x \qquad \text{(PC)}.$$

By MT6,

$$\vdash \Box((B_1 \wedge \ldots \wedge B_n) \supset \Box A^b/x).$$

So

$$\vdash (\forall K,x)\Box((B_1 \wedge \ldots \wedge B_n) \supset \Box A) \qquad \text{(MT9)}.$$

(Note that neither b nor a free x occurs in $B_1,\ldots,B_n$.) Hence by MT10,

$$\vdash (B_1 \wedge \ldots \wedge B_n) \supset \Box(\forall K,x)A.$$

Since $B_1,\ldots,B_n \in \Gamma$,

$$\Gamma \vdash \Box(\forall K,x)A.$$

MT 12

(i) $\vdash (\forall K,x)(K[x] \supset A) \equiv (\forall K,x)A$, provided x is not free in K.
(ii) $\vdash (\exists K,x)(K[x] \wedge A) \equiv (\exists K,x)A$, provided x is not free in K.
(iii) $\vdash (\forall K,x)((\forall K,y)A \supset A^x/y)$, provided x is not free in K and that it is free for y in A.
(iv) $\vdash (\forall K,x)A \equiv \sim(\exists K,x) \sim A$.
(v) $\vdash K[t] \supset .A^t/x \supset (\exists K,x)A$, provided t is free for x in A.
(vi) $\vdash (\forall K,x)(A \supset (\exists K,x)A)$, provided x is not free in K.
(vii) $\vdash (\forall K,x)(A^x/y \supset (\exists K,y)A)$, provided x is not free in K and that it is free for y in A.
(viii) $\vdash (\exists K,x)A \supset .(\forall K,x)(A \supset C) \supset C$, provided x is not free in C.
(ix) $\vdash K(t) \supset (\exists K,x)(K[x] \wedge x = t)$, provided x is not free in K.
(x) $\vdash x = y \supset y = x$.
(xi) $\vdash (\forall K,x)(\forall K,y)(x = y \supset \Box x = y)$.
(xii) $\vdash (\forall K,x)(\forall K,y)(\Diamond x = y \supset \Box x = y)$.
(xiii) $\vdash (\forall K,x)(\forall K,y)(\Diamond x \neq y \supset \Box x \neq y)$.
(xiv) $\vdash \Box s = t \supset .A^s/x \equiv A^t/x$, provided s and t are free for x in A.
(xv) $\vdash K(t) \supset .(\forall K,y)A \supset A^t/y$, provided t is free for y in A and no free occurrence of y falls within the scope of a $\Box$.
(xvi) $\vdash (\exists K,x)(A \wedge B) \equiv (\exists(K,x)A,x)B$

(xvii) $\vdash (\forall(K,x)A,y)B^y/x \equiv (\forall K,x)(A \supset B)$, provided y is free for x in B and B^y/x and B are alphabetic variants (see MT7).

(xviii) $\vdash (\exists(K,x)A,y)B^y/x \equiv (\exists K,x)(A \wedge B)$, provided x, y, B, and B^y/x are related as in (xvii).

(xix) $\vdash (K[c] \wedge A^c/x) \equiv (K,x)A[c]$.

(xx) $\vdash (\exists! K,x)x = x \supset .K[t] \supset t = \text{ɿ}K$.

(xxi) $\vdash (\exists! K,x)K[x] \equiv (\exists! K,x)x = x$, provided x is not free in K.

§3. Completeness of C_1

The soundness of C_1 is easily established in view of Facts 1(ii, iii), (chapter 1, §6) and metatheorems 2, 6, and 7 of chapter 1. We use Fact 1(ii) to establish that AS4 is valid; Fact 1(iii) for AS6; MT2 for AS9; MT6 for AS12; and MT7 for AS7. The rest of the axiom schemata can be shown to be valid quite easily without the aid of semantic metatheorems. Further, modus ponens clearly preserves truth. Hence C_1 is strongly sound in the sense that if $\Gamma \vdash A$, then $\Gamma \vDash A$.

The remainder of this section is devoted to establishing the strong completeness of C_1. We show that C_1 is strongly complete in the following sense: if Γ is a *theory* and A is a *closed* formula, then $\Gamma \vdash A$ if $\Gamma \vDash A$.[3] We introduce several concepts pertaining to theories.

Definition 1. A theory Γ is *complete* iff every closed formula A or its negation $\sim A$ belongs to Γ.

Definition 2. A theory Γ is *proper* iff, if a formula $\sim (\forall K,x)A \in \Gamma$, then $\sim A^b/x \in \Gamma$ and $K[b] \in \Gamma$ for at least one constant b.

Definition 3. A theory Γ is *regular* iff Γ is consistent, complete, and proper.

Definition 4. Γ is an *extension* of Δ iff $\Delta \subseteq \Gamma$.

We now state, but do not prove, Lindenbaum's lemma for C_1. The proof is straightforward (see Hunter (1971)).

Lemma 1. Every consistent theory has a consistent and complete extension.

We prove the completeness of C_1 by showing that every consistent theory is true in some model of L_1. We show this by giving a procedure

3. C_1 is complete in this stronger sense also: if Γ is a set of formulas and A is any formula (open or closed), then $\Gamma \vdash A$ if $\Gamma \vDash A$.

that for each consistent theory yields a model in which it is true. The construction of the model proceeds in several stages. We show first that every consistent theory can be enriched in a certain way, provided denumerably many new constants are added to the language (§3.1). Then, by Lindenbaum's lemma, we obtain a complete extension of this theory. In terms of this new theory, we define a model for enriched L_1 (§3.2). Finally (in §3.3), we show that all members of the consistent theory we began with are true in the model just defined.[4]

§3.1. Let Γ be an arbitrary consistent theory of L_1. In this section we enrich Γ in a certain way. First, add to L_1 denumerably many new constants $c_1, c_2, \ldots, c_n$. (We suppose that the constants are ordered.) Let the new language be L_1^+. It can be shown easily that Γ is a consistent theory of L_1^+ (i.e., of the calculus C_1^+).

Let $\mathscr{W}'$ be an enumeration of all the closed formulas of L_1^+. Define $\mathscr{W}$ to be the enumeration such that

$$\mathscr{W}_1 = \phi$$

and

$$\mathscr{W}_{n+1} = \mathscr{W}'_n.$$

That is, $\mathscr{W}$ is the sequence ϕ, $\mathscr{W}'_1$, $\mathscr{W}'_2, \ldots$. Further, let $\mathscr{X}$ be an enumeration of all the closed formulas of L_1^+ of the form $(\forall K,x)A$. Given $\mathscr{W}$ and $\mathscr{X}$ we obtain an ordering of all the pairs $\langle \mathscr{W}_i, \mathscr{X}_j \rangle$. Let this ordering be $\mathscr{O}$.
Then

$$\mathscr{O}_m = \langle \mathscr{W}_{i_m}, \mathscr{X}_{j_m} \rangle.$$

Define now a sequence of formulas $\mathscr{A}_k$ thus:

$$\mathscr{A}_k = \sim (\forall K,x)B \supset (\sim B^c/x \wedge K[c])$$
$$\text{if } \mathscr{O}_k = \langle \phi, (\forall K,x)B \rangle,$$

and

$$\mathscr{A}_k = \Diamond C \supset \Diamond (C \wedge (\sim (\forall K,x)B \supset (\sim B^c/x \wedge K[c])))$$
$$\text{if } \mathscr{O}_k = \langle C, (\forall K,x)B \rangle,$$

4. The method used here to show the completeness of C_1 is due essentially to Henkin (1949), where the completeness of first order functional calculus is established. Henkin's method has been applied to modal logics by Kaplan (1966), Hughes and Cresswell (1968), and Thomason (1970), among others.

where in either case c is the first constant not to occur in any earlier $\mathscr{A}_i (i < k)$ or in either member of $\mathscr{O}_k$. We use the sequence $\mathscr{A}_1, \mathscr{A}_2, \ldots, \mathscr{A}_k, \ldots$ to define a sequence of theories $\Gamma_0, \Gamma_1, \ldots$ as follows:

$$\Gamma_0 = \Gamma$$

and

$$\Gamma_{n+1} = \Gamma_n \cup \{\mathscr{A}_{n+1}\}.$$

Further, let $\Gamma^\infty = \bigcup_{0 \leq i} \Gamma_i$. We show now that each Γ_i in the sequence is consistent. From this, the consistency of Γ^∞ follows trivially.

Lemma 2. Each Γ_i in the above sequence is consistent.

Proof of Lemma 2. By weak mathematical induction.

Basis. Γ_0 is consistent since $\Gamma_0 = \Gamma$, and Γ is consistent by hypothesis.

Inductive Clause. Suppose as induction hypothesis that Γ_j is consistent. We show that Γ_{j+1} is consistent.

Suppose for reductio that Γ_{j+1} is inconsistent. Then

$$\Gamma_j \vdash \sim \mathscr{A}_{j+1} \qquad \text{(MT4 and PC).}$$

Case I

$$\mathscr{A}_{j+1} = \sim (\forall K, x) B \supset (\sim B^c/x \wedge K[c]),$$

where c has no occurrences in Γ_j, B or k.

So

$$\Gamma_j \vdash \sim (\forall K, x) B \qquad \text{(PC)}$$

and

$$\Gamma_j \vdash \sim (\sim B^c/x \wedge K[c]) \qquad \text{(PC).}$$

That is,

$$\Gamma_j \vdash K[c] \supset B^c/x \qquad \text{(PC).}$$

Hence

$$\Gamma_j \vdash (K[x] \supset B)^c/x^5 \qquad \text{(MT7 and MT8).}$$

Now by MT9 we get

$$\Gamma_j \vdash (\forall K, x)(K[x] \supset B).$$

So

$$\Gamma_j \vdash (\forall K, x) B \qquad \text{(MT12(i)).}$$

This makes Γ_j inconsistent, thus contradicting our induction hypothesis.

5. Note that $K[c] \supset B^c/x$ is not always the same formula as $(K[x] \supset B)^c/x$ (see Definition 3(ii), chapter 1).

Case II

$$\mathscr{A}_{j+1} = \Diamond C \supset \Diamond(C \wedge (\sim (\forall K,x)B \supset (\sim B^c/x \wedge K[c]))),$$

where c has no occurrences in Γ_j, B, or C.

Since

$$\Gamma_j \vdash \sim \mathscr{A}_{j+1},$$
$$\Gamma_j \vdash \Diamond C \qquad (1)$$

and

$$\Gamma_j \vdash \Box \sim (C \wedge (\sim (\forall K,x)B \supset (\sim B^c/x \wedge K[c])) \qquad \text{(PC and S5).}$$

So

$$\Gamma_j \vdash \Box(C \supset (\sim (\forall K,x)B \wedge (K[c] \supset B^c/x))) \qquad \text{(PC and S5).}$$

Hence

$$\Gamma_j \vdash \Box(C \supset \sim (\forall K,x)B) \qquad (2)$$

and

$$\Gamma_j \vdash \Box(C \supset (K[c] \supset B^c/x)) \qquad \text{(PC and S5).}$$

MT7 and the replacement theorem now yield that

$$\Gamma_j \vdash \Box(C \supset (K[x] \supset B))^c/x.$$

Hence

$$\Gamma_j \vdash \Box(\forall K,x)(C \supset (K[x] \supset B))$$
(MT11; clearly all the conditions are met).

Since x is not free in C, we get by AS8, AS9, and S5 that

$$\Gamma_j \vdash \Box(C \supset (\forall K,x)(K[x] \supset B)).$$

So

$$\Gamma_j \vdash \Box(C \supset (\forall K,x)B)$$
(MT12(i) and replacement theorem). (3)

Formulas (2) and (3) yield

$$\Gamma_j \vdash \Box(C \supset ((\forall K,x)B \wedge \sim (\forall K,x)B)) \qquad \text{(S5).}$$

Thus

$$\Gamma_j \vdash \Box \sim C \qquad \text{(S5).}$$

But by (1),

$$\Gamma_j \vdash \Diamond C,$$

making Γ_j inconsistent.

We conclude that each Γ_j and hence Γ^∞ is consistent.

§3.2. Lindenbaum's lemma assures us that every consistent theory has a consistent and complete extension. Let Γ^+ be a consistent complete extension of Γ^∞.

Lemma 3. If Δ is a complete and consistent theory and A is a closed formula, then $A \in \Delta$ iff $\Delta \vdash A$.

This lemma, whose proof is straightforward, yields

Lemma 4. Γ^+ is proper and hence regular.

Definition 5. Let Γ and Δ be theories. Then

$$\Gamma \mathbb{R} \Delta \text{ iff } \{\Box A : \Box A \in \Gamma\} = \{\Box A : \Box A \in \Delta\}.$$

Now let $\mathbf{W} = \{\Delta : \Delta$ is regular and $\Gamma^+ \mathbb{R} \Delta\}$. We can now state and prove the crucial lemma of this section.

Lemma 5. Let $\Delta \in \mathbf{W}$ and $\Diamond A \in \Delta$. Then there is a theory $\Delta' \in \mathbf{W}$ such that $A \in \Delta'$.

Proof of Lemma 5. Since $\Diamond A \in \Delta$, we know that $\Box \Diamond A \in \Delta$ (S5). Hence $\Box \Diamond A$ and $\Diamond A$ both belong to Γ^+. Let $\Sigma = \{\Box B : \Box B \in \Gamma^+\}$. We now define a sequence of theories $\Sigma_1, \ldots, \Sigma_n$ and a sequence of formulas $\mathscr{C}_1, \mathscr{C}_2, \ldots, \mathscr{C}_n$. We define the sequence of formulas first. The definition uses the ordering $\mathscr{X}$ (see p. 54) of formulas of L_1^+ of the form $(\forall K,x)B$.

We let

$$\mathscr{C}_1 = A,$$

and we define

$$\mathscr{C}_{n+1} = \sim (\forall K,x)B \supset (\sim B^c/x \wedge K[c]),$$

where $\mathscr{X}_n = (\forall K,x)B$ and c is the constant for which the formula

$$\Diamond (\mathscr{C}_1 \wedge \mathscr{C}_2 \wedge \ldots \wedge \mathscr{C}_n) \supset \Diamond (\mathscr{C}_1 \wedge \mathscr{C}_2 \wedge \ldots \wedge \mathscr{C}_n \wedge (\sim (\forall K,x)B \supset (\sim B^c/x \wedge K[c])))$$

belongs to the sequence $\mathscr{A}_k$ (defined on p. 54) and hence to Γ^∞ and Γ^+.

Since $\Diamond A (= \Diamond \mathscr{C}_1)$ belongs to Γ^+, it is obvious that for all $n \geq 1$,

$$\Diamond (\mathscr{C}_1 \wedge \mathscr{C}_2 \wedge \ldots \wedge \mathscr{C}_n) \in \Gamma^+ \qquad (1).$$

Now we define recursively the sequence $\Sigma_1, \Sigma_2, \ldots, \Sigma_n$

$$\Sigma_1 = \Sigma \cup \{A\} = \Sigma \cup \{\mathscr{C}_1\}$$

and

$$\Sigma_{n+1} = \Sigma_n \cup \{\mathscr{C}_{n+1}\}.$$

Let

$$\Sigma^\infty = \bigcup_{1 \leq i} \Sigma_i.$$

We show that each Σ_i, and hence Σ^∞, is consistent. Suppose for reductio that Σ_n is inconsistent. Then

$$\Sigma_{n-1} \vdash \sim \mathscr{C}_n \qquad \text{(MT4, PC).}$$

So

$$\Sigma_{n-2} \vdash (\mathscr{C}_{n-1} \supset \sim \mathscr{C}_n) \qquad \text{(deduction theorem),}$$
$$\Sigma_{n-2} \vdash \sim (\mathscr{C}_{n-1} \wedge \mathscr{C}_n) \qquad \text{(PC).}$$

Similarly,

$$\Sigma_{n-3} \vdash \sim (\mathscr{C}_{n-2} \wedge \mathscr{C}_{n-1} \wedge \mathscr{C}_n).$$

By repeating this process we get

$$\Sigma_1 \vdash \sim (\mathscr{C}_2 \wedge \mathscr{C}_3 \wedge \ldots \wedge \mathscr{C}_n)$$

and

$$\Sigma \vdash \sim (\mathscr{C}_1 \wedge \mathscr{C}_2 \wedge \ldots \wedge \mathscr{C}_n).$$

(If $n = 1$, the process gives us $\Sigma \vdash \sim \mathscr{C}_1$.)

Now Σ is modally closed. So

$$\Sigma \vdash \Box \sim (\mathscr{C}_1 \wedge \mathscr{C}_2 \wedge \ldots \wedge \mathscr{C}_n).$$

Therefore,

$$\Gamma^+ \vdash \Box \sim (\mathscr{C}_1 \wedge \ldots \wedge \mathscr{C}_n),$$

since $\Sigma \subseteq \Gamma^+$.

But in view of (1), this makes Γ^+ inconsistent.

This establishes that Σ^∞ is consistent. Let Σ^+ be a consistent and complete extension of Σ^∞. It is easy to see that Σ^+ is proper and hence regular. Equally obviously, $\Gamma^+ \mathbb{R} \Sigma^+$ and $A \in \Sigma^+$. So Lemma 5 is established.

Using **W**, we now define a model for L_1^+. In §3.3 we show that all members of Γ^+ are true in this model. The model **M**, to be defined, is an ordered quintuple $\langle \mathbf{W}, \mathbf{D}, \mathbf{i}^*, \mathbf{m}, \boldsymbol{\rho} \rangle$. **W** is as above. That is,

$$\mathbf{W} = \{\Delta : \Delta \text{ is regular and } \Gamma^+ \mathbb{R} \Delta\}.$$

Further,

$$\boldsymbol{\rho} = \Gamma^+.$$

Designate the set of *closed* terms of L_1^+ by *Term*. Define on *Term* the relation $\equiv_{\Delta}$ ($\Delta \in \mathbf{W}$) as follows:

$$t_1 \equiv_{\Delta} t_2 \text{ iff } t_1 = t_2 \in \Delta.$$

Since

$$\vdash t_1 = t_1,$$
$$\vdash t_1 = t_2 \supset t_2 = t_1,$$

and

$$\vdash t_1 = t_2 \supset (t_2 = t_3 \supset t_1 = t_3),$$

$\equiv_{\Delta}$ is an equivalence relation for each Δ. We represent the partition of *Term*, relative to $\equiv_{\Delta}$, by $Term/\equiv_{\Delta}$. We define $\mathbf{D}$ to be the function which assigns to each "world" Δ, $Term/\equiv_{\Delta}$. That is,

$$\mathbf{D}(\Delta) = Term/\equiv_{\Delta}.$$

Let

$$\mathbf{U} = \bigcup_{\Delta \in \mathbf{W}} \mathbf{D}(\Delta).$$

Further, let $\mathrm{I}_{\Delta}(t)$ be the unique member of $Term/\equiv_{\Delta}$ to which t belongs. (We use I_{Δ} to define $\mathbf{i}^*$ and $\mathbf{m}$.) The following lemma concerning I_{Δ} is obvious.

Lemma 6. $t_1 = t_2 \in \Delta$ iff $\mathrm{I}_{\Delta}(t_1) = \mathrm{I}_{\Delta}(t_2)$ iff $t_2 \in \mathrm{I}_{\Delta}(t_1)$ iff $t_1 \in \mathrm{I}_{\Delta}(t_2)$.

$\mathbf{i}^*$ is the function that assigns to each member Δ of $\mathbf{W}$, $\mathrm{I}_{\Delta}(\text{1}(K,x)x \neq x)$, where K is the first basic noun and x is the first variable.

$\mathbf{m}$ is the function that assigns

(i) to each constant b a function $\mathbf{m}(b)$ from $\mathbf{W}$ into $\mathbf{U}$ such that

$$\mathbf{m}(b)(\Delta) = \mathrm{I}_{\Delta}(b);$$

(ii) to each n-place predicate F, an n-ary relation on $\langle \mathbf{W}, \mathbf{D}, \mathbf{i}^* \rangle$, $\mathbf{m}(F)$, which meets the condition that $\langle \mathbf{d}_1, \ldots, \mathbf{d}_n \rangle \in \mathbf{m}(F)(\Delta)$ iff there are terms $t_1, \ldots, t_n$ such that $\mathrm{I}_{\Delta}(t_i) = \mathbf{d}_i (1 \leq i \leq n)$ and $F(t_1, \ldots, t_n) \in \Delta$;

(iii) to each atomic common noun K an intensional property $\mathbf{m}(K)$ on $\langle \mathbf{W}, \mathbf{D}, \mathbf{i}^* \rangle$ such that an individual concept $\mathbf{i} \in \mathbf{m}(K)(\Delta)$ iff there is a constant c such that $\mathbf{m}(c) = \mathbf{i}$ and $K[c] \in \Delta$.

We show that the intensional property $\mathbf{m}(K)$ assigned to an atomic common noun is separated. (It is easy to verify that the quintuple $\langle \mathbf{W}, \mathbf{D}, \mathbf{i}^*, \mathbf{m}, \rho \rangle$, specified above, meets all the other requirements on models of L_1^+.) Suppose, then, that individual concepts $\mathbf{i}_1$ and $\mathbf{i}_2$ belong to $\mathbf{m}(K)$ at some worlds:

$$\mathbf{i}_1 \in \mathbf{m}(K)(\mathbf{\Delta}_1)$$

and

$$\mathbf{i}_2 \in \mathbf{m}(K)(\mathbf{\Delta}_2).$$

Suppose also that $\mathbf{i}_1(\mathbf{\Delta}) = \mathbf{i}_2(\mathbf{\Delta})$. (We show that $\mathbf{i}_1 = \mathbf{i}_2$.)
From the definition of $\mathbf{m}$ we infer that there are constants c_1, c_2 such that $\mathbf{m}(c_1) = \mathbf{i}_1$ and $\mathbf{m}(c_2) = \mathbf{i}_2$ and

$$K[c_1] \in \mathbf{\Delta}_1$$

and

$$K[c_2] \in \mathbf{\Delta}_2.$$

Hence

$$\Box \Diamond K[c_1] \in \mathbf{\Delta}_1$$

and $\Box \Diamond K[c_2] \in \mathbf{\Delta}_2$ (S5 and Lemma 3).

From the definition of $\mathbf{W}$ we conclude that

$$\Box \Diamond K[c_1], \Box \Diamond K[c_2] \in \mathbf{\Delta}.$$

So

$$\Diamond K[c_1], \Diamond K[c_2] \in \mathbf{\Delta} \qquad \text{(S5)}.$$

Since $\mathbf{i}_1(\mathbf{\Delta}) = \mathbf{i}_2(\mathbf{\Delta}) = \mathbf{m}(c_1)(\mathbf{\Delta}) = \mathbf{m}(c_2)(\mathbf{\Delta})$,

$$\mathbf{I}_{\mathbf{\Delta}}(c_1) = \mathbf{I}_{\mathbf{\Delta}}(c_2) \qquad \text{(definition of } \mathbf{m}\text{)}.$$

Hence

$$c_1 = c_2 \in \mathbf{\Delta} \qquad \text{(Lemma 6)}.$$

Using AS13, we conclude that

$$\Box c_1 = c_2 \in \mathbf{\Delta}.$$

Hence

$$\Box c_1 = c_2 \in \mathbf{\Sigma} \qquad \text{where } \mathbf{\Sigma} \text{ is any member of } \mathbf{W}.$$

So

$$\mathbf{I}_{\mathbf{\Sigma}}(c_1) = \mathbf{I}_{\mathbf{\Sigma}}(c_2) \qquad \text{at all } \mathbf{\Sigma} \in \mathbf{W}.$$

Hence

$$\mathbf{i}_1 = \mathbf{i}_2.$$

§3.3. We show in this section that Γ^+ is true in $\mathbf{M}$.

Lemma 7. (Valuation and membership lemma.) Let α be any closed expression of L_1^+. Then

(i) If α is a formula, $V_{\mathbf{M}}^{\Delta}(\alpha) = T$ iff $\alpha \in \boldsymbol{\Delta}$.
(ii) If α is a term, $V_{\mathbf{M}}^{\Delta}(\alpha) = I_{\Delta}(\alpha)$.
(iii) If α is a common noun, then an individual concept $\mathbf{i} \in V_{\mathbf{M}}^{\Delta}(\alpha)$ iff there is a constant c such that $\mathbf{m}(c) = \mathbf{i}$ and $\alpha[c] \in \boldsymbol{\Delta}$.

Proof of Lemma 7. By strong mathematical induction. Suppose as hypothesis of induction that the lemma holds for all expressions shorter than α. We show that the lemma holds for α, too.
Case 1. α is an atomic closed term. So α is a constant. The lemma holds by the definition of **m** and MT5(i) (chapter 1).
Case 2. α is an atomic common noun. Trivially from MT5(ii) (chapter 1) and the definition of **m**.
Case 3. α is the formula $t_1 = t_2$. Since α is closed, t_1 and t_2 are closed, too. Applying the induction hypothesis, we get

$$V_{\mathbf{M}}^{\Delta}(t_1) = I_{\Delta}(t_1)$$

and

$$V_{\mathbf{M}}^{\Delta}(t_2) = I_{\Delta}(t_2).$$

But

$$I_{\Delta}(t_1) = \mathbf{I}_{\Delta}(t_2) \text{ iff } t_1 = t_2 \in \boldsymbol{\Delta} \qquad \text{(Lemma 6).}$$

Hence

$$V_{\mathbf{M}}^{\Delta}(t_1) = V_{\mathbf{M}}^{\Delta}(t_2) \text{ iff } t_1 = t_2 \in \boldsymbol{\Delta}.$$

So

$$V_{\mathbf{M}}^{\Delta}(t_1 = t_2) = T \text{ iff } t_1 = t_2 \in \boldsymbol{\Delta} \qquad \text{(MT5(iii), chapter 1).}$$

Case 4. α is the formula $F(t_1, \ldots, t_n)$. Again $t_1, \ldots, t_n$ are closed and the induction hypothesis yields that

$$V_{\mathbf{M}}^{\Delta}(t_i) = I_{\Delta}(t_i) \qquad (1 \leq i \leq n).$$

Now suppose that $F(t_1, \ldots, t_n) \in \boldsymbol{\Delta}$. Then by definition of **m**, $\langle \mathbf{I}_{\Delta}(t_1), \ldots, \mathbf{I}_{\Delta}(t_n) \rangle \in \mathbf{m}(F)(\boldsymbol{\Delta})$. Hence $\langle V_{\mathbf{M}}^{\Delta}(t_1), \ldots, V_{\mathbf{M}}^{\Delta}(t_n) \rangle \in \mathbf{m}(F)(\boldsymbol{\Delta})$. By MT5(iv) (chapter 1), we get $V_{\mathbf{M}}^{\Delta}(F(t_1, \ldots, t_n)) = T$.

Suppose, on the other hand, that $V_{\mathbf{M}}^{\Delta}(F(t_1, \ldots, t_n)) = T$. The induction hypothesis yields that $\langle I_{\Delta}(t_1), \ldots, I_{\Delta}(t_n) \rangle \in \mathbf{m}(F)(\boldsymbol{\Delta})$. Using the definition of **m**, we conclude that there are terms $s_1, \ldots, s_n$ such that $I_{\Delta}(s_i) = I_{\Delta}(t_i)$, $(1 \leq i \leq n)$, and

$$F(s_1, \ldots, s_n) \in \boldsymbol{\Delta}.$$

By Lemma 6, we get that

$$s_i = t_i \in \mathbf{\Delta} \qquad (1 \leq i \leq n).$$

Hence

$$F(t_1, \ldots, t_n) \in \mathbf{\Delta} \qquad \text{(AS11 and Lemma 3).}$$

Case 5. α is the formula $\sim A$. Trivial.
Case 6. α is the formula $(A \supset B)$. Trivial.
Case 7. α is $\Box A$.

Suppose that $\Box A \in \mathbf{\Delta}$. Then $\Box A \in \mathbf{\Sigma}$, for all $\mathbf{\Sigma} \in \mathbf{W}$ (definition of $\mathbf{W}$). By Lemma 3, $A \in \mathbf{\Sigma}$, and by the induction hypothesis, $V_{\mathbf{M}}^{\Sigma}(A) = T$. Now MT5(vii) (chapter 1) yields that $V_{\mathbf{M}}^{\Delta}(\Box A) = T$.

Suppose that $V_{\mathbf{M}}^{\Delta}(\Box A) = T$. And suppose, for reductio, that $\Box A \notin \mathbf{\Delta}$. Since $\mathbf{\Delta}$ is complete, $\sim \Box A \in \mathbf{\Delta}$. So $\Diamond \sim A \in \mathbf{\Delta}$. Hence by Lemma 5, there is a theory $\mathbf{\Delta}' \in \mathbf{W}$ such that $\sim A \in \mathbf{\Delta}'$. Since $\mathbf{\Delta}'$ is consistent $A \notin \mathbf{\Delta}'$. By the induction hypothesis we now get $V_{\mathbf{M}'}^{\Delta'}(A) \neq T$. Hence $V_{\mathbf{M}}^{\Delta}(\Box A) \neq T$ (MT5(vii), chapter 1). And this contradicts our first assumption.
Case 8. α is $(\forall K, x)A$.

Suppose that $(\forall K, x)A \in \mathbf{\Delta}$, and suppose, for reductio, that $V_{\mathbf{M}}^{\Delta}((\forall K, x)A) \neq T$. Hence there is an assignment $\mathbf{a}'$ normal in $\mathbf{\Delta}$ for which

$$V_{\mathbf{M},\mathbf{a}'}^{\Delta}((\forall K, x)A) \neq T.$$

So there is an assignment $\mathbf{a}$ that is $\mathscr{S}$ variant of $\mathbf{a}'$ at x in $\mathbf{\Delta}$ such that

$$V_{\mathbf{M},\mathbf{a}}^{\Delta}(A) \neq T,$$

where $\mathscr{S}$ is a function that assigns to each $\mathbf{\Sigma}$, $V_{\mathbf{M}}^{\Sigma}(K)$. (Clearly $\mathscr{S}$ is a sort for $\langle \mathbf{W}, \mathbf{D}, \mathbf{i}^* \rangle$.)

Consider now the unique individual concept $\mathbf{i} \in V_{\mathbf{M}}^{\Delta}(K)$ such that $\mathbf{i}(\mathbf{\Delta}) = \mathbf{a}_0(x)$. The definition of $\mathbf{a}$ assures us that there is such a concept $\mathbf{i}$. Since $\mathbf{i} \in V_{\mathbf{M}}^{\Delta}(K)$ and K is a closed common noun, we get from the induction hypothesis that there is an individual constant c such that $\mathbf{m}(c) = \mathbf{i}$ and $K[c] \in \mathbf{\Delta}$. So by MT5(viii) (chapter 1),

$$V_{\mathbf{M}}^{\Delta}(K[c]) = T.$$

Clearly the conditions for MT7 (chapter 1) are now met. So we conclude that

$$V_{\mathbf{M},\mathbf{a}}^{\Delta}(A^c/x) \neq T.$$

Hence

$$\mathrm{V}^{\boldsymbol{\Delta}}_{\mathbf{M}}(A^c/x) \neq \mathrm{T}.$$

By the induction hypothesis,

$$A^c/x \notin \boldsymbol{\Delta}.$$

But $(\forall K,x)A$ and $K[c] \in \boldsymbol{\Delta}$, contradicting the regularity of $\boldsymbol{\Delta}$.

Suppose, on the other hand, that $\mathrm{V}^{\boldsymbol{\Delta}}_{\mathbf{M}}((\forall K,x)A) = \mathrm{T}$ and suppose, for reductio, that $(\forall K,x)A \notin \boldsymbol{\Delta}$. Since $\boldsymbol{\Delta}$ is complete,

$$\sim (\forall K,x)A \in \boldsymbol{\Delta}.$$

And since $\boldsymbol{\Delta}$ is proper, there is an individual constant c such that

$$\sim A^c/x, K[c] \in \boldsymbol{\Delta}.$$

By the induction hypothesis,

$$\mathbf{m}(c) \in \mathrm{V}^{\boldsymbol{\Delta}}_{\mathbf{M}}(K).$$

So by MT5(viii) (chapter 1),

$$\mathrm{V}^{\boldsymbol{\Delta}}_{\mathbf{M}}(K[c]) = \mathrm{T}.$$

Further, since $\boldsymbol{\Delta}$ is consistent, $A^c/x \notin \boldsymbol{\Delta}$. So by the induction hypothesis,

$$\mathrm{V}^{\boldsymbol{\Delta}}_{\mathbf{M}}(A^c/x) \neq \mathrm{T}.$$

Now let $\mathbf{a}$ be an assignment normal in $\boldsymbol{\Delta}$ such that $\mathbf{a}_0(x) = \mathbf{m}(c)(\boldsymbol{\Delta})$ and $\mathbf{a}_s(x) = \mathscr{S}$, where $\mathscr{S}$ is a function that assigns to each world $\boldsymbol{\Sigma}$, $\mathrm{V}^{\boldsymbol{\Sigma}}_{\mathbf{M}}(K)$. Clearly, there is at least one such assignment. Now we may apply MT7 (chapter 1) to get

$$\mathrm{V}^{\boldsymbol{\Delta}}_{\mathbf{M},\mathbf{a}}(A) \neq \mathrm{T}.$$

But this contradicts our first assumption that

$$\mathrm{V}^{\boldsymbol{\Delta}}_{\mathbf{M}}((\forall K,x)A) = \mathrm{T}.$$

Case 9. α is $(K,x)A$.

Suppose that

$$\mathbf{i} \in \mathrm{V}^{\boldsymbol{\Delta}}_{\mathbf{M}}((K,x)A).$$

Then

$$\mathbf{i} \in \mathrm{V}^{\boldsymbol{\Delta}}_{\mathbf{M},\mathbf{a}}((K,x)A),$$

where **a** is any assignment normal in **Δ**. The definition of V (p. 40) yields

$$\mathbf{i} \in V^{\Delta}_{\mathbf{M},\mathbf{a}}(K) \qquad (1)$$

and

$$V^{\Delta}_{\mathbf{M},\mathbf{a}'}(A) = T \qquad (2)$$

where $\mathbf{a}' \underset{x}{=} \mathbf{a}$ and $\mathbf{a}'_0(x) = \mathbf{i}(\Delta)$ and $\mathbf{a}'_s(x) = \mathscr{S}$. $\mathscr{S}$ is a function that assigns to each $\boldsymbol{\Sigma} \in \mathbf{W}$, $V^{\Sigma}_{\mathbf{M}}(K)$. From (1), using the induction hypothesis, we get that there is an individual constant c such that $\mathbf{i} = \mathbf{m}(c)$ and $K[c] \in \boldsymbol{\Delta}$. Also, $V^{\Delta}_{\mathbf{M}}(K[c]) = T$ (MT5(viii), chapter 1). Formula (2) and MT7 now yield that

$$V^{\Delta}_{\mathbf{M},\mathbf{a}'}(A^c/x) = T.$$

Since A^c/x is closed,

$$V^{\Delta}_{\mathbf{M}}(A^c/x) = T.$$

Applying the induction hypothesis we get

$$A^c/x \in \boldsymbol{\Delta}.$$

Hence $(K,x)A[c] \in \boldsymbol{\Delta}$, since both $K[c]$ and A^c/x belong to $\boldsymbol{\Delta}$ (MT12(xix)).

Suppose, on the other hand, that there is a constant c such that $\mathbf{m}(c) = \mathbf{i}$ and $\alpha[c] \in \boldsymbol{\Delta}$. By MT12(xix), $K[c]$ and A^c/x belong to $\boldsymbol{\Delta}$. Clearly, K and A^c/x are both closed. So by the induction hypothesis,

$$\mathbf{i} \in V^{\Delta}_{\mathbf{M}}(K)$$

and

$$V^{\Delta}_{\mathbf{M}}(A^c/x) = T.$$

Consider an assignment **a**, normal in **Δ**, such that $\mathbf{a}_0(x) = \mathbf{i}(\boldsymbol{\Delta})$ and $\mathbf{a}_s(x) = \mathscr{S}$, where $\mathscr{S}$ is a function that assigns to each world $\boldsymbol{\Sigma}$, $V^{\Sigma}_{\mathbf{M}}(K)$. Clearly, there is such an assignment **a**. Since $V^{\Delta}_{\mathbf{M}}(K[c]) = T$, we can apply MT7 (chapter 1) to get

$$V^{\Delta}_{\mathbf{M},\mathbf{a}}(A) = T.$$

The definition of V yields

$$\mathbf{i} \in V^{\Delta}_{\mathbf{M},\mathbf{a}}((K,x)A).$$

Since $(K,x)A$ is closed,

$$\mathbf{i}\in \mathrm{V}_{\mathbf{M}}^{\Delta}((K,x)A) \qquad \text{(MT3, chapter 1).}$$

Case 10. α is ιK.

Either (a) there is a unique concept $\mathbf{i}\in \mathrm{V}_{\mathbf{M}}^{\Delta}(K)$ or (b) there is not such a unique concept.

Suppose first that there is the unique concept $\mathbf{i}$. Then, by the induction hypothesis, there is a constant c such that $\mathbf{m}(c)=\mathbf{i}$ and $K[c]\in\mathbf{\Delta}$. Now suppose, for reductio, that $\sim(\exists! K,x)x=x\in\mathbf{\Delta}$. That is,

$$\sim(\exists K,y)(\forall K,x)(x=x\equiv x=y)\in\mathbf{\Delta},$$

where y is the first variable distinct from x. (See Definition 2(vi), chapter 1.) From MT12(iv), AS7, and the replacement theorem we get that

$$\sim(\forall K,x)(x=x\equiv x=c)\in\mathbf{\Delta}.$$

Since $\mathbf{\Delta}$ is proper, there is a constant c' such that

$$K[c']\in\mathbf{\Delta} \qquad (1)$$

and

$$\sim(c'=c'\equiv c'=c)\in\mathbf{\Delta}.$$

Hence

$$c'\neq c\in\mathbf{\Delta} \qquad \text{(PC and regularity of } \mathbf{\Delta}\text{).}$$

So

$$\mathbf{m}(c')=\mathbf{i}'\neq\mathbf{i}=\mathbf{m}(c).$$

But from (1), $\mathbf{i}'\in \mathrm{V}_{\mathbf{M}}^{\Delta}(K)$ by an application of the induction hypothesis. This contradicts the assumption that there is a unique individual concept belonging to $\mathrm{V}_{\mathbf{M}}^{\Delta}(K)$. We conclude, therefore, that

$$(\exists! K,x)x=x\in\mathbf{\Delta},$$

and this together with the fact that $K[c]\in\mathbf{\Delta}$ yields

$$c=\iota K\in\mathbf{\Delta}.$$

Hence

$$\mathrm{I}_{\Delta}(c)=\mathrm{I}_{\Delta}(\iota K).$$

But

$$\mathrm{I}_{\Delta}(c)=\mathbf{i}(\mathbf{\Delta})=\mathrm{V}_{\mathbf{M}}^{\Delta}(\iota K) \qquad \text{(MT5(xix), chapter 1).}$$

Therefore, $V_{\mathbf{M}}^{\Delta}(\urcorner K) = I_{\Delta}(\urcorner K)$.

Suppose, on the other hand, that there is not a unique concept belonging to $V_{\mathbf{M}}^{\Delta}(K)$. And suppose, for reductio, that $V_{\mathbf{M}}^{\Delta}(\urcorner K) \neq I_{\Delta}(\urcorner K)$. But $V_{\mathbf{M}}^{\Delta}(\urcorner K) = \mathbf{i}^*(\mathbf{\Delta})$ (MT5(xix), chapter 1.) So $I_{\Delta}(\urcorner K) \neq \mathbf{i}^*(\mathbf{\Delta})$. Hence

$$\urcorner K = \urcorner(K', x)x \neq x \notin \mathbf{\Delta}$$

where K' is the first basic common noun and x is the first variable (Lemma 6 and the definition of $\mathbf{i}^*$). Regularity of $\mathbf{\Delta}$ and AS15 now yield that $(\exists ! K, x)x = x \in \mathbf{\Delta}$. That is,

$$(\exists K, y)(\forall K, x)(x = x \equiv x = y) \in \mathbf{\Delta}.$$

Since $\mathbf{\Delta}$ is proper, there is a constant c such that

$$K[c] \in \mathbf{\Delta}$$

and

$$(\forall K, x)(x = x \equiv x = c) \in \mathbf{\Delta}.$$

Applying the induction hypothesis to K, we get that $\mathbf{m}(c) \in V_{\mathbf{M}}^{\Delta}(K)$. Since $V_{\mathbf{M}}^{\Delta}(K)$ does not have a unique member, there is an individual concept $\mathbf{i}$ such that $\mathbf{m}(c) \neq \mathbf{i}$ and $\mathbf{i} \in V_{\mathbf{M}}^{\Delta}(K)$. Separation of sorts implies that $\mathbf{i}(\mathbf{\Sigma}) \neq \mathbf{m}(c)(\mathbf{\Sigma})$ at all $\mathbf{\Sigma} \in \mathbf{W}$. And by the induction hypothesis we get that there is a constant c' such that $\mathbf{m}(c') = \mathbf{i}$ and $K[c'] \in \mathbf{\Delta}$. Since $\mathbf{m}(c')(\mathbf{\Delta}) \neq \mathbf{m}(c)(\mathbf{\Delta}), c' = c \notin \mathbf{\Delta}$. But $(\forall K, x)(x = x \equiv x = c)$ and $K[c'] \in \mathbf{\Delta}$. Therefore,

$$c' = c' \equiv c' = c \in \mathbf{\Delta} \qquad \text{(AS7 and regularity of } \mathbf{\Delta}).$$

Hence

$$c' = c \in \mathbf{\Delta}, \text{ thus yielding a contradiction.}$$

This completes the proof of Lemma 7.

So Γ^+ is true in $\mathbf{M}$. Hence Γ, from which Γ^+ was constructed, is also true in $\mathbf{M}$. Now $\mathbf{M}$ is a model of L_1^+. By appropriate restrictions it can be turned into a model of L_1, and it is easily shown that Γ is true in the new model, too. So we conclude:

Main Theorem. Every theory consistent according to the calculus C_1 is true in some model of L_1.

C_1, then, is strongly complete.

3 Necessity and Existence

Language L_1, presented in chapter 1, was constructed on the premise that its common nouns pick out necessary existents. Thus if K is a common noun of L_1, it is required that a K that exists in one possible situation exists in all possible situations countenanced by the language. This premise has a very restrictive effect on the applicability of L_1: either the common nouns of L_1 have to be restricted to those like 'number' or 'set', or the possibilities countenanced by L_1 have to be restricted severely. In this chapter I explore some of the ways in which a more general conception of common nouns can be accommodated in a logic of quantifiers and modality.

Section 1 develops a more general theory of the intensions of common nouns than was offered in chapter 1, §5. In §2, I examine some of the ways in which this conception of common nouns can be fitted in a logic of quantifiers and modality. The technical problems in this area are more difficult than may appear at first sight. These problems result in the development of a number of different theories. In §3, I compare the resulting systems with modal systems proposed by other authors. Finally, in §4, I consider briefly some philosophically interesting extensions of the systems presented in this and previous chapters.

§ *1. Semantics of Common Nouns*

We have seen that common nouns differ from predicates in that they have associated with them, as part of their intension, a *principle of identity.* A common noun such as 'man' divides all objects (in a world and at a particular time) into those of which it is true and those of which it is false; and in this respect it resembles predicates. These, too, have associated with them, as part of their intension, a *principle of application.* But common nouns have more to their intension than a mere principle of application. The common noun 'man', for instance, provides a principle for determining when an object at time t (and/or world w) is *the same man* as an object at time t′ (and/or world w′). Predicates do not provide such a principle of identity. This fact, Geach has observed, is reflected in the grammar of 'the same'.

An adequate theory of the intensions of common nouns, then, must represent both a principle of application and a principle of identity. In chapter 1, we represented these intensions by intensional properties (see Definition 8, chapter 1). We understood the intensional properties in the following way: if $\mathscr{I}$ represents the intension of a common noun *K* and the individual concept i belongs to $\mathscr{I}$ at w, i.e., $i \in \mathscr{I}(w)$, then i(w) is a *K* in w and i(w′) in w′ is the same [*K*] as i(w) in w. This has the consequence that all common nouns pick out necessary existents. If a *K* exists in one world, it exists in all the worlds countenanced by the language. This is so because individual concepts are total functions. They are defined at all the worlds. So if i(w) is a *K* in w, then i(w′) is well defined, and by definition it is the same [*K*] in w′ as i(w) is in w. That is, the [*K*] that i(w) is in w exists at every world w′.

There are several equally natural ways of dealing with this. We can modify our definition of intensional properties so that they assign to each world a set of *partial concepts*. In this picture, if the concept i belongs to the intension of *K* at w and i is undefined at w′, then i(w) is a *K* in w but this *K* does not exist in w′. Another way is to use some object to mark nonexistence. I develop the second approach here, and I use i*(w) (see p. 19) to mark nonexistence in w. Now intensions of common nouns are again represented by intensional properties, but with the following understanding.

Proposition 1. Suppose that $\mathscr{I}$ represents the intension of a common noun *K* and that $i \in \mathscr{I}(w)$. Then i(w) is a *K* in w if $i(w) \neq i^*(w)$. And also, i(w) in w is the same [*K*] as i(w′) in w′ if $i(w') \neq i^*(w')$. Otherwise, this [*K*] does not exist in w′.

Illustration. Suppose, for simplicity, that there are only three worlds, w_1, w_2, and w_3; that the objects a, b, c, * exist in all these worlds; that * represents nonexistence in each of the worlds; and, finally, that 'man born in Jerusalem' has as its intension $\mathscr{I}$:

$\mathscr{I}$:

w_1	w_2	w_3
ab*	ab*	
b*c		
c**		

Now we understand $\mathscr{I}$ as encoding the following information. First, a, b, and c are all men born in Jerusalem in w_1. The first man exists in w_2 but not in w_3; the second in w_3 but not in w_2; and the third man exists only in w_1. Of these men only the first is born in Jerusalem in w_2, and none is born in Jerusalem in w_3.

Given our new understanding of intensional properties, it is clear that the intensions of common nouns should not be required to be separated (Definition 10, chapter 1). There is a world in which both Nixon and Ford do not exist. Hence there is a world in which the Nixon-concept (i_N) and the Ford-concept (i_F) coincide. That is, for some w,

$$i_N(w) = i_F(w) = i^*(w).$$

But of course we cannot and should not identify i_F with i_N. The old concept of separation should be replaced by the concept of *near separation.* Let $\mathfrak{A}(= \langle W, D, i^* \rangle)$ be a model structure (Definition 4, chapter 1).

Definition 1. An intensional property $\mathscr{I}$ is *nearly separated* in $\mathfrak{A}$ iff all individual concepts i, i′ that belong to $\mathscr{I}$ at some worlds (i.e., $i \in \mathscr{I}(w_1)$ and $i \in \mathscr{I}(w_2)$, for some $w_1, w_2 \in W$) are such that if $i(w) = i'(w) \neq i^*(w)$ at any world w, then $i = i'$.

We require the intensions of common nouns to be nearly separated. (For motivation of this requirement see the discussion of separation on pp. 28–33.) We call the intensions of common nouns '*sorts*'.

Definition 2. $\mathscr{I}$ is a *sort* in a model structure $\mathfrak{A}$ iff $\mathscr{I}$ is an intensional property in $\mathfrak{A}$ and $\mathscr{I}$ is nearly separated in $\mathfrak{A}$.[1]

Definition 3. An intensional property $\mathscr{I}$ is *nearly constant* in $\mathfrak{A}$ iff,

1. A plausible additional requirement on sorts is this: if $\mathscr{I}$ is a sort and $i \in \mathscr{I}(w)$, then $i(w) \neq i^*(w)$.

if an individual concept i belongs to $\mathscr{I}$ at any world w, then i belongs to $\mathscr{I}$ at all worlds w′ such that $i(w') \neq i^*(w')$.

Definition 4. $\mathscr{I}$ is a *substance sort* in $\mathfrak{A}$ iff $\mathscr{I}$ is a sort in $\mathfrak{A}$ and $\mathscr{I}$ is nearly constant in $\mathfrak{A}$.[2,3]

The new notion of "substance sort" is a generalization of the notion defined in chapter 1. Whereas previously only "number", "number greater than three", and the like counted as substance sorts, now 'man', 'river', etc., also express substance sorts. Nouns that express substance sorts will be called *substance nouns*. Such nouns give essential properties of objects that fall under them.

We define some concepts that will prove useful in the following section. We use '$\mathscr{S}$', '$\mathscr{S}'$', and '$\mathscr{S}_1$' to range over sorts (of a fixed model structure $\mathfrak{A}$).

Definition 5. $\mathscr{S}[w] = \{d:\ d \in D(w)$ and $d \neq i^*(w)$ and there is an individual concept $i \in \mathscr{S}(w)$ such that $i(w) = d\}$.

2. The concept of "substance sort" is similar to Bressan's notion of "quasi-absoluteness" (Bressan (1972), p. 94), but the two are not identical. Quasi-absoluteness is a world-relative attribute of intensional properties. An intensional property may be quasi-absolute in one world but not in another. Substance sort is not similarly world relative. That is, substance sort is modally constant (in Bressan's sense) but quasi-absoluteness is not. Since Bressan does not mention this, I prove the claim by example. Consider the intensional property $\mathscr{I}$ displayed below. (Suppose that in our model structure there are only two worlds, w_1, w_2, and that only two objects b and the "nonexisting" object * exist in these worlds.)

$\mathscr{I}$:

w_1	w_2
bb	bb *b

It is obvious that $\mathscr{I}$ is nearly constant (or, in Bressan's terminology, it is quasi-modally constant in every world). But $\mathscr{I}$ is quasi-modally separated only in w_1. Hence $\mathscr{I}$ is quasi-absolute in w_1 but not in w_2. That is, quasi-absoluteness is not modally constant.

Similarly, my concept of "near separation" and Bressan's concept of "quasi-modal separation" are, though closely connected, not identical. The connection between them is this: $\mathscr{I}$ is nearly separated if and only if $\mathscr{I}^{\cup}$ is quasi-modally separated in every (any) world. (See note 18, chapter 1.)

3. Henceforth when I use the expressions 'sort' and 'substance sort', I shall mean these in the sense of Definitions 2 and 4, respectively. When I mean these in the sense of chapter 1, I shall say explicitly 'sort in the sense of chapter 1' and 'substance sort in the sense of chapter 1'.

Definition 6. $\mathscr{S}[\![w]\!] = \{d: d \in D(w)$ and $d \neq i^*(w)$ and there is an individual concept $i \in \mathscr{S}(w')$, for some $w' \in W$, such that $i(w) = d\}$.

Definition 7. d *in* w *is the same* $\mathscr{S}$ *as* d′ *in* w′ iff $d \neq i^*(w)$ and $d' \neq i^*(w')$ and there is an individual concept i which belongs to $\mathscr{S}$ at some world and $i(w) = d$ and $i(w') = d'$.

Definition 8. The $\mathscr{S}$ *counterpart in* w′ *of the individual* d *in* w (abbreviated to $\mathscr{S}(w',d,w)$) is the unique individual d′ such that d′ in w′ is the same $\mathscr{S}$ as d in w.

These definitions are similar to Definitions 14–17 of chapter 1. For the intuitive motivation of the definitions consider Proposition 1 above, and see pages 35–36.

§2. *Semantics of Necessity*

Let L_2 be a modal language whose syntax is exactly like that of L_1 except, for simplicity, we drop "restriction" (Definition 1(vii), chapter 1) and descriptions. Further, common nouns of L_2 are understood as expressing *nearly separated* intensional properties. We examine in this section various ways of interpreting L_2.

We can adopt for the most part the semantics of L_1 given in chapter 1, §§6, 7; but the clause for necessity (□) needs further consideration. Our initial intuition concerning □ was this: an object d of the sort $\mathscr{S}$ satisfies □ Fx in w iff d satisfies Fx in w and *the same* $\mathscr{S}$ in any other world w′ satisfies Fx in w′. (We used the sort to determine which object in w′ is the same $\mathscr{S}$ as d in w.) Since our sorts are now *nearly* separated intensional properties, a *K* that exists in one world may not exist in another. Hence our initial intuition requires some development. Our fundamental problem is to decide how nonexistence will be treated in the semantics of necessity.

First Approach. The most natural development of our initial intuition is that a *K* satisfies □ Fx in w iff it satisfies Fx in w and it satisfies Fx in any world w′ in which it exists. Or, more formally, an object d of the sort $\mathscr{S}$ satisfies □ Fx in w iff d satisfies Fx in w, and at all worlds w′ at which $\mathscr{S}(w',d,w)$ (see Definition 8) is defined, $\mathscr{S}(w',d,w)$ satisfies Fx in w′. Essentially, this intuition will be developed in the first approach. But, first, we need to decide under what conditions two (or more) objects bear a relation *R* essentially. That is, under what conditions do two $\mathscr{S}$'s, say d_1 and d_2, bear the relation $\Box Rxy$? Should we consider those worlds in which both exist, or those in which at least one exists? Our intuitions concerning *de re* modality do not seem to favor one approach over the other. We follow the first alternative: the two $\mathscr{S}$'s, d_1 and d_2, bear the relation $\Box Rxy$ iff they bear the relation R in all the worlds in which they both exist.

We adopt all the standard definitions of model, assignment, etc., given in chapter 1 (Definitions 18–22), except that the expression 'sort' in these definitions is understood to mean "sort according to Definition 2 of chapter 3." We can also adopt much of the definition of satisfaction of §7, chapter 1.

Definition 9. Clauses (i)–(vii) as in Definition 24, chapter 1.

(viii) If α is the formula $\Box$A, then $V^{w}_{M,a}(\alpha) = T$ if $V^{w'}_{M,f(w',a,w)}(A) = T$ *at all worlds w′ at which f(w′,a,w) is defined.* Otherwise, $V^{w}_{M,a}(\alpha) = F$.

(ix) If α is the formula $(\forall K,x)A$, then $V^{w}_{M,a}(\alpha) = T$ if $V^{w}_{M,a'}(A) = T$ for all assignments a′ that are m(K) variants of a at x in w.

(Clauses (x) and (xi) of Definition 24 are irrelevant because L_2 does not have restriction and descriptions.)

This definition of satisfaction is a natural extension of the semantics of L_1 along the intuitions expressed earlier. But it has some very undesirable consequences. I suppose that the worst consequence is the failure of the semantic metatheorem MT2 (chapter 1, §10) for L_2. The satisfaction conditions of a formula A at an assignment depend on what the assignment assigns to *all* the variables and not just those that occur free in A. This results in the invalidity of the schemata

(1) $K[x] \supset .(\forall K,x)A \supset A$

(2) $A \supset (\forall K,x)A$ (x is not free in A).

Further, not all closed formulas A are such that either $M \models A$ or $M \models \sim A$.

I will not prove that all these claims hold for the semantics of L_2, but I will illustrate the invalidity of (2). Let the model $M = \langle W, D, i^*, m, \rho \rangle$ be as follows: $W = \{w, w'\}$; D assigns to each world $\{1,2,*\}$; i* is **; $\rho = w$; and let m assign to the constant b the individual concept 11, to the one-place predicate F the property P, and to the common noun K, the sort $\mathscr{S}$.

P:

w	w′
1	2

$\mathscr{S}$:

w	w′
11	11

Let a assign to each variable the object 1 and to all variables except x, the sort $\mathscr{S}$. Let it assign $\mathscr{S}'$ to x.

$\mathscr{S}'$:

w	w′
1*	*2

It is easy to verify that, by Definition 9,

$$V^{w}_{M,a}(\Box Fb) = T,$$

but

$$V^{w}_{M,a}((\forall K,x)\Box Fb) = F.$$

Hence,

$$V^{w}_{M,a}(\Box Fb \supset (\forall K,x)\Box Fb) = F.$$

Failure of axiom schemata (1) and (2) makes the semantics of L_2, as given in Definition 9, very unattractive. Variables, in this semantics, take on a mysterious character, and our formulas end up saying things that we never intended them to say. (Here, I think, we have a nice illustration of how syntax can illuminate semantics. The definition of satisfaction is perfectly coherent, and it gives well-defined conditions of truth, and hence meaning, to the formulas of L_2. But the definition is unacceptable, nonetheless. And its unacceptability becomes quite obvious once we consider syntactic matters, such as axiomatization of the valid formulas.)

Axiom schemata (1) and (2) fail because clause (viii) (Definition 9) makes the values of all the variables relevant to the satisfaction conditions of a formula $\Box A$. Clause (viii) requires us to consider only those worlds w′ at which f(w′,a,w) is defined. And whether f(w′,a,w) is defined depends on *all* the variables, not just on those that occur free in A. Note, however, that when evaluating $\Box A$ at a world relative to an assignment, we *need* not shift the values of all the variables; we need shift only the values of those variables that occur free in A. This maneuver, it appears, will get around the earlier failure of MT2 and the consequent invalidity of (1) and (2). Care, however, must be exercised. The idea, naively instituted, will falsify the modal law,

$$\Box(A \supset B) \supset . \Box A \supset \Box B.$$

The second approach develops the idea in a more sophisticated way.

The Second Approach. Here the free variables in a formula are made explicit by the rules of formation. We define the notion of formula (of L_3) thus.

Definition 10

(i) Let F be an n-place predicate and $t_1,\ldots,t_n$ any terms and let $x_1,\ldots,x_m$ be a list of variables that contain all the variables among $t_1,\ldots,t_n$ and in which no variable is repeated.[4] Further, let $K_1,\ldots,K_m$ be a list of common nouns. Then $(x_1K_1,\ldots,x_mK_m)$ $F(t_1,\ldots,t_n)$ is a formula. (The list $x_1K_1,\ldots,x_mK_m$ may be empty.)

(ii) Let $t_1,\ldots,t_n$ and $x_1,\ldots,x_m$ and $K_1,\ldots,K_m$ be as before. Then $x_1K_1,\ldots,x_mK_m)t_1 = t_2$ is a formula.

(iii) If $(x_1K_1,\ldots,x_mK_m)A$ is a formula, then so are $(x_1K_1,\ldots,$ $x_mK_m) \sim A$, $(x_1K_1,\ldots,x_{m-1}K_{m-1})(\forall K_m, x_m)A$, and $(x_1K_1,\ldots,$ $x_mK_m)\Box A$.

(iv) If $(x_1K_1,\ldots,x_mK_m)A$ and $(x_1K_1,\ldots,x_mK_m)B$ are formulas, then $(x_1K_1,\ldots,x_mK_m)(A \supset B)$ is a formula.

A *well-formed formula* (wff) of L_3 is a formula of the form $(\ )A$. That is, a wff has no "free" variables.

I will now sketch the semantics of L_3 without giving technical details. Definition of model is as before but assignments assign to variables only objects. The $(x_1K_1,\ldots,x_mK_m)$ variant of an assignment a in a world w′ relative to w is the assignment a′ obtained by shifting the values a assigns to $x_1,\ldots,x_m$, appropriately. For example, a′ will assign to x_1, $\mathrm{m}(K_1)(\mathrm{w}',\mathrm{a}(x_1),\mathrm{w})$ if this is defined (Definition 8).

The satisfaction conditions for all formulas are as you would expect. In particular, an assignment a satisfies $(x_1K_1,\ldots,x_mK_m)\Box A$ at w if at all worlds w′ at which the $(x_1K_1,\ldots,x_mK_m)$ variant of a (a′) is

4. The list $x_1, \ldots, x_m$ may contain variables not occurring among $t_1, \ldots, t_n$. If the list is required to contain *only* those variables that occur among $t_1, \ldots, t_n$, then the list of variables that precedes any "formula" will contain all and only free variables in that formula. This requirement complicates the syntax and the semantics of $\supset$. It becomes difficult even to get modus ponens to be a valid inference pattern.

defined, a′ satisfies $(x_1 K_1, \ldots, x_m K_m)A$ in w′. Truth is understood as satisfaction by all assignments.

The analogue of MT2 (chapter 1, §10) holds for L_3. The satisfaction conditions of a formula depend only on the values assigned to the "free" variables of the formula. (By "free" variables of a formula I mean the variables that precede it.) But (alas!) the analogue of schema (2),

(3) $(\ldots)(A \supset (\forall K,x)A)$,

is still invalid. This is so because the "free" variables of the two occurrences of *A* are not the same.

Language L_3 is much better behaved than L_2, but it still leaves a lot to be desired. The main argument against L_3 is that it is cumbersome and hence not very usable. I know of no *elegant and simple* way of constructing a semantics of necessity that (i) fits with the intuition expressed on pages 71–72 and (ii) yields the "right" logical truths. In the third approach, I drop the first requirement, and the system that results is quite simple and usable.

The Third Approach. In this approach we consider *all* the worlds when computing the truth value of $\Box Fx$. Roughly, the semantics of $\Box$ is now this: an object d of the sort $\mathscr{S}$ satisfies $\Box Fx$ in w iff at every world w′, d′ satisfies Fx in *w*′, where d′ is $\mathscr{S}$ (w′,d,w) if it is defined; otherwise, d′ is i*(w′). Care has to be exercised in the way this semantics is formulated because, otherwise, the S4 law,

$$\Box A \supset \Box\Box A,$$

will fail. It turns out that this law can be preserved and the semantics simplified if variables are assigned individual concepts.

Details. Let L_4 be a language whose syntax is the same as the syntax of L_1. (L_4 has restriction and descriptions.) Model structures and models are defined as before. The notion of *assignment* and other related notions need to be defined anew.

Definition 11. An *assignment* for L_4 relative to a model M(= ⟨W,D,i*,m,ρ⟩) is a function that assigns to each variable of L_4 an individual concept in ⟨W,D,i*⟩.

Definition 12. An assignment a′ *is an* $\mathscr{S}$(w) *variant of* a *at x in* w iff (i) $a' \underset{x}{\doteqdot} a$, (ii) $a'(x) \in \mathscr{S}(w)$, and (iii) $a'(x)(w) \neq i^*(w)$.

Definition 13. (Definition of satisfaction for L_4.) Let M(=

$\langle W, D, i^*, m, \rho \rangle$) be a model, $w \in W$, and a an assignment relative to M. We define recursively the valuation function V:

(i) If α is a constant, then $V^{w}_{M,a}(\alpha) = m(\alpha)(w)$.

(ii) If α is a variable, then $V^{w}_{M,a}(\alpha) = a(\alpha)(w)$.

(iii) If α is a common noun, then $V^{w}_{M,a}(\alpha) = m(\alpha)(w)$.

(iv)–(vii) Clauses for predication, $=, \sim, \supset$, are standard.

(viii) If α is $\Box A$, then $V^{w}_{M,a}(\alpha) = T$ if $V^{w'}_{M,a}(A) = T$ at all worlds $w' \in W$. Otherwise, $V^{w}_{M,a}(\alpha) = F$.

(ix) If α is $(\forall K, x)A$, then $V^{w}_{M,a}(\alpha) = T$ if $V^{w}_{M,a'}(A) = T$ at all assignments a′ that are $V^{w}_{M,a}(K)$ variants of a at x in w. Otherwise, $V^{w}_{M,a}(\alpha) = F$.

(x) If α is the common noun $(K, x)A$, then $V^{w}_{M,a}(\alpha)$ is the set of individual concepts i that satisfy the following condition: $i \in V^{w}_{M,a}(K)$ and $V^{w}_{M,a'}(A) = T$, where $a' \underset{x}{\simeq} a$ and $a'(x) = i$.

(xi) If α is the term $\urcorner K$, then $V^{w}_{M,a}(\alpha)$ is the value of i at w if i is the unique individual concept belonging to $V^{w}_{M,a}(K)$. Otherwise, $V^{w}_{M,a}(\alpha) = i^*(w)$.

Logical concepts for L_4 are defined as before.

The analogue of MT2 (chapter 1, §10) holds for L_4. Satisfaction conditions of a formula A depend only on the values of variables free in A. Also, schemata (1) and (2) are valid in L_4. In fact, all the axiom schemata AS1–AS16 of chapter 2 are valid except for

$$\text{AS13.} \quad \Diamond K[t_1] \wedge \Diamond K[t_2] \supset .t_1 = t_2 \supset \Box t_1 = t_2.$$

This axiom schema is invalid because common nouns in L_4 are assigned *nearly* separated intensional properties. (*Reminder:* Common nouns in L_1 were assigned separated intensional properties.) A weaker version of AS13,

$$\text{AS13*.} \quad \Diamond K[t_1] \wedge \Diamond K[t_2] \supset .t_1 = t_2 \supset .t_2 \neq \urcorner(K', y)y \neq y \supset \Box t_1 = t_2,$$

is valid in L_4. I believe that with the other axiom schemata, AS13* provides a complete calculus for L_4.[5]

5. I have not yet verified all the details of the completeness proof.

We can define in L_4 the concept of existence and also the concept of substance sort. These are given the following metalinguistic definitions.

Definition 14. $E(t) = \mathrm{Df} \sim t = \rceil(K,x)x \neq x$, where K is the first common noun and x is the first variable.

Definition 15. K is a substance sort $= \mathrm{Df}\,\Box(\forall K,x)\Box(E(x) \supset K(x))$. Note that the Barcan formula and the converse Barcan formula,

$$(\forall K,x)\Box Fx \supset \Box(\forall K,x)Fx,$$
$$\Box(\forall K,x)Fx \supset (\forall K,x)\Box Fx,$$

are invalid in L_4 even when K is restricted to substance nouns. That is, the formulas

(4) K is a substance sort $\supset .(\forall K,x)\Box Fx \supset \Box(\forall K,x)Fx$,

(5) K is a substance sort $\supset .\Box(\forall K,x)Fx \supset (\forall K,x)\Box Fx$

are invalid in L_4. Invalidity of (4) fits well with our intuitions, but the invalidity of (5) does not. The reason for the divergence between our intuitions and L_4 is this. In L_4, when evaluating whether a K fulfills the condition

$$\Box Fx,$$

we consider all the worlds, but intuitively we consider only those worlds in which that K exists. A weaker version of (5),

(6) K is a substance sort $\supset .\Box(\forall K,x)Fx \supset (\forall K,x)\Box(Ex \supset Fx)$,

is valid in L_4.

Variables in L_4 are assigned individual concepts; but in L_1, variables are assigned objects and sorts. Is this a significant difference? I am inclined to believe that the difference is of little philosophical significance. As I see it, the role of the assignments in L_1 and L_4 is the same—to assign values to the variables *and* to trace these values through various worlds according to some principles of identity. In L_1 this job is performed by the ordered pairs (consisting of an object and a sort), which are associated with the variables; in L_4 the same job is done by the individual concepts. Assignments in L_1 and L_4 are quite different kinds of entities, but they serve the same function. *Warning*: We must not interpret the assignments as giving the "value of the variables," in Quine's sense of this phrase. (If this interpretation were correct, then the difference between L_1 and L_4 would indeed be philosophically significant.) Assignments in our languages do not (merely) give the objects of which the open sentences are true. Thus in L_1 the variables are assigned ordered pairs. But the sentence

$$Fx$$

of L_1 is not (necessarily) true of an ordered pair. Similarly, in L_4 open sentences are *not* true of individual concepts. In L_4 we are not "quantifying over" individual concepts; sentences of L_4 are not about individual concepts.

§3. Comparisons

The most distinctive feature of the modal logics developed here is that they treat common nouns and predicates as belonging to different logical categories. Both syntactically and semantically, the behavior of common nouns in our logics is very different from the behavior of predicates. Common nouns combine with determiners (i.e., quantifiers and the description operator), but predicates do not; common nouns supply a principle of identity but, again, predicates do not.

The logics developed here bear a superficial resemblance to the theories of sortal quantification proposed by Wallace (1965) and others.[6] In these theories, too, a sharp distinction is drawn between sortals (i.e., substance nouns) and predicates. But the differences between sortals and predicates in these theories turn out to be primarily syntactic; there are no significant differences in their semantics. Thus in these systems sortal quantification is eliminable in favor of unrestricted quantification, and the logics appear to be mere notational variants of the standard first order logic. In a way this is not surprising. For sortals, and more generally common nouns, have a distinctive semantic role only in the intensional contexts; in the extensional contexts, the principles of identity they supply do not come into play.

Our logics have a deeper kinship with Bressan's ML^{ν} (1972). Bressan does not make a logical or categorial distinction between common nouns and predicates. Common nouns are for him special kinds of predicates. He is able, nevertheless, to represent the semantic difference between common nouns and predicates. He is able to do this because

6. In particular, Leslie Stevenson. See Stevenson (1975) and also his more recent paper, Stevenson (1977).

predication in Bressan's logic is *intensional.* That is, the truth value of a subject–predicate sentence in Bressan's logic depends in general on the intension of the subject term. Thus predicates in the first-order fragment of ML^{ν} express intensional properties; they are true or false of individual concepts. And common nouns in Bressan are special kinds of intensional predicates—those that express "absolute" (i.e., separated and modally constant) intensional properties. Thus while Bressan treats common nouns as predicates, still the important semantic difference between them remains. Common nouns express a principle of application *and* a principle of identity, but predicates express only the former. Bressan offers, as far as I know, the first adequate formal theory of common nouns.

There are some differences between the logics I advocate and Bressan's ML^{ν} which deserve mention. First, common nouns in my theory are not special kinds of predicates. The role of common nouns in L_1–L_4 is quite different from the role of all predicates, extensional or intensional (see §4). Second, a bare quantifier on my theory makes no sense. It needs to be supplemented with a common noun. Third, predication in L_1–L_4 is extensional. Predication in Bressan, as I have remarked, is intensional. This has some undesirable consequences. Bressan is forced to speak of a "double use" of common nouns—their use as extensional concepts and their use as absolute concepts. This "double use" is best seen by way of an example. Consider

(7) Necessarily the top card is a card,

(8) Some card is necessarily the top card.

According to Bressan, 'card' expresses, on the one hand, an absolute concept (or a quasi-absolute concept if we take into account existence). It is true of those individual concepts which, so to speak, pick out the same card. On the other hand, 'card' also expresses an extensional concept: it is true in a world w of all those individual concepts which pick out a card in w. The extensional concept must be employed in the translation of (7), for the-top-card-concept belongs to 'card' only on the extensional reading. In (8), however, the first occurrence of 'card' must express the absolute concept. On the most natural reading, (8) is false; but if 'card' is understood extensionally, it will turn out true because the-top-card-concept does fulfill the condition "being necessarily the top card." Bressan translates (7) and (8) thus:

(9) $\Box C^{e}(t)$,
(10) $(\exists x)(C^{a}(x) \wedge \Box x = t)$.

Here C^{e} and C^{a} express, respectively, the extensional and the absolute concepts of 'card'. And t stands for the term 'the top card'.

In L_1–L_4 the apparent double use of 'card' is seen to be due to a difference in scope. In (7) 'card' has narrow scope, but in (8) it has wide scope. Examples (7) and (8) are represented by

(11) $\Box(\exists C,x)x = t$,
(12) $(\exists C,x)\Box x = t$,

respectively. C stands for the common noun 'card' and t, as before, for the term 'the top card'.

The fourth difference between ML^{v} and L_1–L_4 concerns their correspondence with natural languages. The most direct way of translating (first-order) ML^{v} into English is to read its quantifiers $(\forall x)$ and $(\exists x)$ as 'every individual concept x is such that' and 'some individual concept x is such that', respectively. Thus (10) says in this scheme that

> Some individual concept x is such that x belongs to C^{a} and x necessarily coincides with t.

Given our intuitive understanding of C^{a} and t, this claim is equivalent to (8). Hence (10) is an adequate translation of (8)—for some purposes anyway. But it must be remarked that in order to translate (8), ML^{v} employs rather rich and intensional concepts. On the other hand, quantifiers of L_1–L_4, $(\forall K,x)$ and $(\exists K,x)$, can be read simply as 'every K, x is such that' and 'some K, x is such that', respectively. The correspondence between (7), (8) and (11), (12) is direct and straightforward. To put the point a bit differently—and in a way that I do not much like—Bressan's translations of (7) and (8) quantify over individual concepts, whereas my translations of these sentences quantify over ordinary objects such as playing cards. I am inclined to view first-order ML^{1} as a special case of the language L_1. First-order ML^{1} is L_1 with just one common noun 'individual concept' ($\boldsymbol{I}$) and one special two-place predicate 'coincide' ($\boldsymbol{O}$) governed by the axiom

$$(\forall \boldsymbol{I},x)(\forall \boldsymbol{I},y)(\Box \boldsymbol{O}xy \equiv x = y).$$

I should note that Hintikka (1969a), Lewis (1971), and Thomason (1973) have also expressed ideas that are in some respects similar to those developed here. Hintikka (1969a) has emphasized that the use of quantifiers, especially in modal contexts, presupposes a "method of individuation." He has argued that two different methods of individuation—a physical method and a perceptual method—are found in our conceptual scheme. Hintikka has further suggested that for each of these methods of individuation there should be a separate quantifier in modal logics, at least insofar as they are used as logics of perception. Although I am not convinced by Hintikka's argument that there is a special perceptual method of individuation, I agree with him that quantifying in makes sense only if a method of individuation (i.e., a principle of identity) is associated with the quantifier. I have argued that common nouns supply the requisite principle of identity.

Thomason (1973) has developed Hintikka's ideas further. He has presented a formal theory that captures at least some of Hintikka's intuitions. This theory is quite similar to the language L_1 of chapter 1.

Lewis (1971) has hinted that different common nouns pick out different principles of identity or, in his terminology, different "counterpart relations." He says, "If we are to have multiple counterpart relations, we may well wonder how many to have. One for every sortal? One for every natural kind? One for every common noun phrase that can grammatically be inserted into 'regarded as ———' ... ? I do not know" (p. 210). Lewis has also proposed a way of modifying counterpart theory to accommodate multiple counterpart relations.

Finally, Kripke (1963) and Thomason (1969) have offered theories of necessity and existence that are very close to the theory developed in the third approach. What differences there are result from the fact that trans-world identity of individuals is left unanalyzed in their systems. I have not seen any discussion of the first two approaches in the literature.

§4. *Some Extensions*

Languages L_1 and L_4 can be extended and modified in many ways. I mention in this section some extensions and modifications that seem to me of especial philosophical interest.

A particularly useful extension of our languages is obtained by adding *intensional predicates.* These predicates behave very much like ordinary predicates except that the truth value of a subject–predicate sentence containing an intensional predicate depends on the *intension* of the subject term. Let Q be a one-place intensional predicate. Then, the formula Qt is true in a world w iff the intension of t (i.e., the individual concept assigned to t) belongs to the extension of Q at w. Note that in L_1 variables, too, have associated with them an individual concept. An assignment a, normal in w, assigns to a variable x a sort $\mathscr{S}$ and an object d which is of the sort $\mathscr{S}$. Now d and $\mathscr{S}$ together determine an individual concept—namely, the one that traces the $\mathscr{S}$ that d is in w through the various possible worlds. I call this individual concept *the intension of* x *relative to* a *in* w. Now, a formula Qx is true relative to an assignment a in w iff the individual concept corresponding to x relative to a in w belongs to the extension of Q at w. The above definition can easily be extended to n-place intensional predicates.

The addition of intensional predication to L_1–L_4 makes them useful for the analysis of certain fragments of natural languages. For instance,

(13) The top card is necessarily the top card.
(Understood *de dicto*.)

and Partee's example,

(14) The temperature is rising,

can naturally be analyzed in terms of intensional predication. In (13) we can treat 'is necessarily the top card' as an intensional predicate true of those individual concepts which in each world pick out a top card. Note that the intensional property expressed by 'is necessarily the top card' is modally constant, but not separated. In (14) 'is rising' expresses an intensional property (in a temporal interpretation of "intensional property" and the rest). This intensional property is neither modally constant nor separated.

What predicates are viewed as intensional depends on the ontology one adopts. Even as blatant an example of intensional predication as (14) can be treated as a case of the standard variety if we reify "the temperature" in a certain way—that is, if we treat "the temperature" as a single temporally extended and evolving object. In this ontology, 'is rising' expresses an ordinary extensional property of temperatures and other such things. Note that this analysis will view the occurrence of 'is' in

The temperature is 85°F

not as one of identity but as one of "coincidence." Thus, by multiplying entities, intensional predication can be reduced to extensional predication. Conversely, ontological reduction can be effected if some predicates, ordinarily viewed as extensional, are treated as intensional. Consider the case of the statue and the clay of which it is made (at a time t). What is the relation between the two? Identity or diversity? Often it is argued that the two could not be identical because whereas it is true to say that

(15) The statue came into existence in August 1975,

yet it is false to say that

(16) The clay came into existence in August 1975.

Hence there is a property which the statue has but which the clay does not. The identity of the statue and the clay, it is argued, conflicts with Leibniz's law. The crucial assumption in such arguments is that predicates like

(17) ...came into existence in August 1975

are extensional. I think it plausible to reject this assumption and to hold, on the contrary, that the truth values of (15) and (16) depend not only on the extensions of 'the statue' and 'the clay' but also on the principles of identity these terms supply; that is, it is plausible to hold that the predicate (17) is intensional. We explain the divergence in the truth values of (15) and (16) not by positing different entities as designata of 'the statue' and 'the clay' but by the fact that these terms supply different principles of identity.

"Intensional predication," I should note, is somewhat of a misnomer. For in intensional predication what matters is the intension of the subject term and the *extension* of the predicate. This type of predication is more accurately called "intensional–extensional predication." The familiar predications, as in

Socrates weighs 170 lb,

are now seen to be of the "extensional–extensional" variety. The two remaining types of predication are possible and can easily enough be added to our logics. These *may* be useful for the analysis of some sentences. For example, in

(18) Jones is essentially rational,

we may view 'is essentially' as signaling extensional–intensional predication. (I am ignoring here the problems of trans-world identity.) An example of the "intensional–intensional" predication is perhaps provided by 'is always' in

The price of eggs is always rising.

In the following pages I stick to the old terminology because it is brief. I will use 'intensional predication' to mean 'intensional–extensional' predication.

Once we have intensional predicates we can dispense with ordinary extensional predicates, at least as a separate logical category. Their role can now be played by special kinds of intensional predicates, namely, those which are "extensional" in every world (see Belnap (1972)). We can take one further step in this direction. We can eliminate common nouns as a distinct logical category also: we can assimilate them with intensional predicates. The system that results is first-order ML^1. The advantages of these moves, as Belnap has emphasized, is the resultant uniformity and simplicity. Common nouns, extensional predicates, and intensional predicates are seen as fundamentally alike. Also, all terms, names, variables, and definite descriptions are treated in exactly the same way. They all take as their semantic values, individual concepts.

Another way of achieving uniformity is this. Instead of treating variables like names and descriptions, we can treat names and descriptions like variables. That is, we now assign to all terms—variables, names, descriptions—an object and a sort. Thus, for example, the semantic value of the name 'Gerald Ford' consists of an object, Gerald Ford, and a sort "person" (or perhaps "man" or "animal"). This idea, I imagine, will be favored by Geach, who has argued that proper names express a "nominal essence."

Definite descriptions create a difficulty. It seems that descriptions such as 'the house in which Jack was born' must be assigned an individual concept and a sort. It is insufficient to associate with it the sort "house" and the actual house in which Jack was born. This semantic representation does not give us all the information we need. For example, it does not tell us the house in which Jack is born in another world w. Thus it appears that we lose uniformity. Names and variables are assigned objects and sorts; but descriptions are assigned individual concepts and sorts. We can reinstate uniformity in two ways: (1) we can assign individual concepts to variables and names also (this proposal is technically easier to implement); or (2) we can assign to a description such as the one above the sort "house in which Jack was born."

Once sorts are assigned to all terms, the next step is to see all predication as attributive. The truth value of a subject–predicate sentence in this type of predication depends, in general, upon the object and the sort assigned to the subject terms. The semantic value of a predicate yields at each world a set of ordered pairs consisting of a sort and an object. Extensional and intensional predication now become special cases of attributive predication. In extensional predication, the sort assigned to the subject term is irrelevant; if $\langle \mathrm{d}, \mathscr{S} \rangle$ belongs to the extension of an extensional predicate F at a world w, then for any sort $\mathscr{S}'$, $\langle \mathrm{d}, \mathscr{S}' \rangle$ also belongs to F at w. Similarly, in intensional predication what matters is the individual concept "corresponding" to the subject term (as determined by the sort and the object); the rest is irrelevant. In the present theory attributive adjectives are not incomplete predicates. Sentences such as

Phaedo is ferocious

express complete thoughts. What these mean ordinarily (not always) is this. Let F be an attributive adjective and let a be a subject term whose "nominal essence" is given by K. Then

a is F

means that

a is F for a K.

4 Essentialism and Trans-World Identity

I consider in this and the following chapter two major objections to modal logics. The first objection, raised by Quine, contends that quantified modal logics are committed to an unacceptable essentialism. I discuss this objection in the present chapter, and I determine how far it applies to the modal logics developed earlier. According to the second objection, modal logics fail to meet Tarski's convention T.[1] I explain and evaluate this objection in chapter 5.

§*1*. *Modal Logics and Essentialism*

Quine's objection to quantified modal logics divides naturally into two parts: (1) that these logics are committed to essentialism, and (2) that essentialism is a false or meaningless doctrine. I leave the discussion of (2) for the next section. In this section I determine how far, and in what sense, modal logics are committed to essentialism. My concern will primarily be with the modal systems presented in the earlier chapters.

Essentialism, as Quine understands it, is the thesis that "some of the attributes of a thing (quite independently of the language in which the thing is referred to, if at all) may be essential to the thing and others accidental" (Quine (1966) pp. 173–74). The essential attributes of a thing are those that it could not have lacked: those attributes that it has in all the possible worlds in which it exists.[2] Its accidental attributes are those that it might have lacked: those that it has in some worlds but not in others. Thus, for example, the property "being greater than seven" is an essential property of nine, whereas the property "numbering the planets" is one of its accidental properties. Quine finds the division of attributes into essential and accidental, "quite independently

1. A more exact formulation of the objection is given in chapter 5.

2. This statement requires modification if we regard "existence" as one of the attributes of objects.

of the language in which the thing is referred to," puzzling and paradoxical, and he claims that modal logics are committed to this division.

Parsons (1969), developing some ideas of Marcus (1967), has clarified the sense in which modal logics are committed to essentialism. He has noted that modal logics (or many of them) entail certain essentialistic claims. Thus

(1) $(\exists x)(\Box(Fx \vee \sim Fx) \wedge \sim \Box(Fx \wedge \sim Fx))$

is a theorem of most (all?) systems of quantified modal logic. But he points out that these essentialistic claims are not problematic. They can be understood quite straightforwardly in terms of modality *de dicto*. Parsons has proposed a formal characterization of the sort of essentialistic claim that Quine finds troublesome, and he has shown that modal logics are not committed to these claims in at least the following two senses: (1) they do not imply these essentialistic claims; that is, these are not among the theorems of the standard systems of modal logic; (2) they do not require that some such claim hold—"in the sense that the system, together with some obvious and uncontroversial nonmodal facts, entails that some such [claim] be true" (Parsons (1969) p. 41). Thus Parsons's investigation shows that quantified modal logics are committed *at most* to the meaningfulness but not the truth of the sort of essentialistic statements that Quine finds troublesome.[3]

That standard systems of modal logics are committed to the meaningfulness of essentialism cannot be denied. For in these systems open sentences such as

(2) $\Box Fx$

are true or false of objects independently of a mode of designation. And this clearly presupposes that it is *meaningful* to mark some of the properties of an object as essential to it and others as accidental. The same holds of various nonstandard systems—for example, Thomason's Q2 and the first-order fragment of Bressan's ML^{ν}. These systems are committed to the meaningfulness of essentialism also, but only for individual concepts. This is so because open sentences in Q2 and (first-order) ML^{ν} are true (or false) of individual concepts.

3. I should note a further claim that is made by Parsons in this connection. He thinks that "freedom of commitment to essentialism in the first two senses *allows* a freedom of any *objectionable* commitment [to the meaningfulness of essentialistic statements]" ((1969) p. 50).

Modal logics L_1–L_4 are *not* committed to the meaningfulness of essentialism. Here formulas like (2) are not true or false of objects—nor of individual concepts—absolutely. Objects fulfill open sentences only relative to a principle of identity. Thus L_1–L_4 are not committed to idea that an object, independently of a principle of identity, has some of its properties essentially and others accidentally.

Essentialistic predications on our view are meaningful, but their logic is quite different from the logic of ordinary predications. Consider, for example,

(3) The number of planets is greater than seven,

(4) The number of planets is essentially greater than seven.

In (3) the description 'the number of planets' is used to refer to the object that actually numbers the planets, nine; but in (4) the role of the description is more complex. It is used to pick out nine and it is also used to trace this number from world to world. There is a corresponding difference in the role of the predicates in (3) and (4). In the former, the predicate 'is greater than seven' expresses a property, and (3) is true if the object picked out by the subject term has the attribute expressed by the predicate. The truth conditions of (4) are as follows: (4) is true iff the object picked out by the subject term is greater than seven and this object as traced by the principle of identity for 'number' is greater than seven in every world. *The important point to note is that the predicate in* (4), '*is essentially greater than seven*', *does not express a property of objects.* This is confirmed by the fact that the context

(5) ——— is essentially greater than seven

is not referentially transparent. Coreference of terms is insufficient to warrant interchangeability in (5): the principles of identity supplied by the terms are also relevant. Curiously, necessary coreference is insufficient to guarantee interchangeability, too. We cannot, in general, infer

The K is essentially F

from

The K' is essentially F

and

Necessarily the K is the K'.

'The K' and 'The K'' can be necessarily coextensive and yet they may supply different principles of identity. Terms are interchangeable *salva veritate* in (5) if they are coextensive *and* if they supply the same principle of identity. I call such contexts *nearly transparent.*

Logics L_1–L_4, I have argued, are not committed to the essential/accidental division of the properties of objects. Essential attribution in L_1–L_4 makes sense only relative to a principle of identity. This I have explained is not inconsistent with our ordinary talk. We can understand ordinary essentialistic claims, e.g., (4), while rejecting the idea that objects have some of their properties necessarily and others contingently.

Our logics are committed to the meaningfulness of relativized essential properties. Thus, although expressions such as

——— is essentially *F*

do not express properties of objects, more complicated predicates, e.g.,

(6) ——— is essentially *F qua K*,

do express properties in L_1–L_4. Predicate (6) can be represented in L_1 thus:

$$(\exists K,x)(\text{———} = x \wedge \Box Fx).$$

Note that the position occupied by '———' is fully transparent (cf. Lewis (1971) and Gibbard (1975)). Properties such as (6) are reminiscent of the essential properties Quine finds unobjectionable (over and above modality *de dicto*). But there is this important difference between the two. In Quine's understanding of relativized essences, for example (6), what is important is the analytic (or *de dicto*) connection between *F* and *K*; in our understanding of these essences, what is important is the principle of identity associated with *K*. Quinean essences can easily be explained in terms of modality *de dicto*. Understood *à la* Quine,

(7) *x* is essentially *G qua F*

is equivalent to

(8) *x* is *F* and necessarily all *F*'s are *G*'s.

Relativized essential properties of the kind to which L_1–L_4 are committed cannot, in the like manner, be paraphrased in terms of modality *de dicto*. Our logics are committed to a deeper grade of essentialism than Quinean essentialism.

We may distinguish, then, three grades of essentialism. The first grade, Quinean essentialism, allows essential predication relative to a mode of designation. It allows us to say of a man, for example, that he is essentially rational *qua* rational animal, but essentially two-legged *qua* featherless biped. This grade of essentialism is no more than a stylistic variant of modality *de dicto*.

The second grade of essentialism, one to which L_1–L_4 are committed, requires essential predications to be relativized to a principle of identity. Mode of designation of the object in this grade of essentialism is unimportant, save for that part that supplies the principle of identity. Thus, although it is true to say (perhaps) of a man that he is essentially rational *qua* rational animal, yet it is false to say of him that he is essentially featherless *qua* featherless animal. This is so even though, as Quine would say, his featherlessness follows just as analytically from 'featherless animal' as does his rationality from 'rational animal'. In this grade of essentialism the analytic connection between F and K is irrelevant to determining the truth of

x is essentially F *qua* K.

What matters is the principle of identity supplied by K.

The third and last grade of essentialism is one to which the standard systems of modal logics are committed. Here essential attribution requires no relativization. We may say of a man that he is essentially rational not merely *qua* man or *qua* animal, but *qua* itself. This grade of essentialism is properly called *Aristotelian essentialism.* It rests on the assumption that for each object there is a sort that answers in the most fundamental way the question, *What is it*? The claim that

x is essentially F

is now understood to mean

(9) x is essentially F *qua* what x is.

The Aristotelian assumption in this grade of essentialism is that for every object x there is a *unique* sort that answers to 'what x is' in (9). The assumption, it may be noted, does not rule out one and the same object from falling under two or more different sorts with different principles of identity. In such a situation the assumption requires that one sort be more fundamental to the object than the others. This final grade of essentialism can be defined by the following equation.

The third grade of essentialism = the second grade
+ the Aristotelian thesis.

Modal logics L_1–L_4 are neutral with respect to Aristotelian essentialism. They are committed neither to its meaningfulness nor to its meaninglessness. The question of its meaningfulness is, however, of some importance. On it rests the admissibility of *unrestricted* quantification. If the Aristotelian thesis is correct, then there is a sense of 'thing' (or 'entity') in which it expresses a sort, and hence unrestricted quantification is meaningful. We noted in chapter 1 the various ways in which 'thing' is employed in English. It is sometimes used as a dummy noun, standing in place of a common noun proper that is understood from the context. Sometimes it is used as a pro–common noun; here it works something like a variable. It has other uses besides; we noted in chapter 1 the great difficulty of giving a uniform and unified account of this word. In any case, if the Aristotelian thesis is correct, we may admit a use of 'thing' in which it is a common noun in its own right. In this use it is true of every object x, and it traces each x across worlds according to the principle of identity determined by what x is. (It is easy to see that if the Aristotelian thesis holds, then on the present definition 'thing' expresses a sort. For if we suppose, for reductio, that 'thing' does not express a sort, that is, that the intension of 'thing' is not separated, then at some world two principles of identity will correspond to some one object. This contradicts the Aristotelian thesis that for each object x (at any world) there is a unique sort that answers what x is.) Formally, the common noun 'thing' (abbreviated to $\boldsymbol{T}$) can be introduced into our modal logics by the axiom schema

(10) $\Box(\forall K,x)(\exists \boldsymbol{T},y)x = y.$

This says in ordinary English that

Necessarily every K is a thing,

and it is clearly a logical truth. Schema (10) cannot be strengthened to

(11) $\Box(\forall K,x)(\exists \boldsymbol{T},y)\Box\, x = y.$

This would be true only if every common noun in the language gives the "nature" of the objects to which it applies. The claim is doubtful for natural languages, and the Aristotelian thesis does not imply it.

If Aristotelian essentialism is meaningful, then unrestricted quantification makes sense and there is (or can be) a use of 'thing' in which it functions as a genuine common noun. Conversely, if 'thing' does function as a common noun, then Aristotelian essentialism is meaningful. For we may understand the unrelativized claim

x is essentially *F*

to mean that

x is essentially *F qua* thing.

The question whether Aristotelian essentialism is meaningful, then, is equivalent to the question whether there is a use of 'thing' in which it expresses a sort, that is, whether 'thing' provides a principle of identity. This last question has aroused some disagreement of late. Kripke (1972) holds (or seems to hold) that 'thing' does supply a principle of identity—that it makes sense to say of objects in different worlds that they are "the same thing." He has argued that doubts about such trans-world identifications rest on a wrong picture about possible worlds—that they are something like distant planets which are given to us qualitatively. Possible worlds, according to Kripke, are not discovered but rather stipulated. What thing is what in a possible world is something we stipulate, not something we discover. And, Kripke argues, stipulation of which individuals are talked about in a possible world is no more objectionable than which qualities are talked about in that possible world. I may note that it is not completely clear that Kripke is talking about 'thing' in the sense under discussion. His examples seem to suggest that he uses 'thing' in a loose and popular way, as a dummy noun standing for a common noun proper. His argument for trans-world identity, then, shows only that identifications such as "the same man" and "the same number" are not problematic in the way that some philosophers have seen them to be. On the other hand, Kripke does use his argument to defend unrestricted quantification.

Gibbard (1975) holds, contrary to Kripke, that 'thing' is not a genuine common noun. He has argued that trans-world identifications *qua* thing do not make sense. "Meaningful cross-world identities of such things as statues ... must be identities *qua* something: *qua* statue or *qua* lump.... It makes sense to talk of the "same statue" in different possible worlds, but no sense to talk of the 'same thing'" (p. 194). Gibbard's argument for this is based on a case of contingent identity.

He constructs an example in which claims (12)–(14) hold:

(12) a in w is the same statue as b in w′,

(13) a in w is the same lump of clay as c in w′,

(14) b and c are distinct in w′.

Now which of the two things b,c in w′ is the "same thing" as a in w? And how do we decide? There seems no coherent way to answer these questions. Hence, Gibbard concludes, the claims of trans-world identity *qua* thing do not make sense. It should be noted that contingent identity establishes conclusively that there is no use of 'thing' which satisfies schema (11). But its bearing on a use that fulfills (10) is less clear.

I will not here decide the question whether there is (or there can be) a use of 'thing' in which it functions as a genuine common noun. But I remark that even if there is such a use and, thus, even if unrestricted quantification is meaningful, the Fregean analyses of restricted quantification in terms of unrestricted quantification are, in any case, incorrect. That is, it is incorrect to analyze

(15) Every K is thus and so,

(16) Some K is thus and so

as

(17) Everything is such that if it is a K,
then it is thus and so,

(18) Something is such that it is a K and it is thus and so,

respectively. These analyses hold only if schema (11) is valid. (Suppose that (11) is invalid. Then for some 'K',

$$(\exists K,x)(\forall \boldsymbol{T},y)\Diamond x \neq y$$

holds true at some world w (in a model). Then by Fregean analyses,

$$(\exists \boldsymbol{T},x)(K(x) \wedge (\forall \boldsymbol{T},y)\Diamond x \neq y)$$

holds at w, too. This conflicts with the law

$$(\forall \boldsymbol{T},x)\boldsymbol{T}[x].)$$

But if (11) is valid, then all identities are necessary. That is, (11) implies

(19) $(\forall K,x)(\forall K',y)(x = y \supset \Box x = y)$.

And this is inconsistent with cases of contingent identity such as the one constructed by Gibbard. Contingent identity, then, provides a strong argument against Fregean analyses. A consequence of our rejection of these analyses is that common nouns

(20) thing that is a K

and

(21) K

are not logically equivalent. Some of Kripke's arguments for mind–body duality, it may be noted, rest on the supposed equivalence of (20) and (21).

§2. The Status of Essentialism: A Problem about Identity

Modal logics L_1–L_4, I have argued, are committed to the second grade of essentialism, but not to Aristotelian essentialism. It remains to be investigated if the second grade of essentialism is philosophically acceptable. There is little in the literature that is *explicitly* addressed to this question. However, many arguments and problems that are raised against Aristotelian essentialism apply equally to the essentialism under consideration. This section is devoted to a detailed discussion of one such problem raised by Chisholm in 1967. This is, in my opinion, one of the most difficult problems about essentialism and trans-world identity brought forward to date. Chisholm's problem, if my suggestion for its solution is correct, shows the need for an important modification in our theory of common nouns.

Before I present Chisholm's problem, I would like to say something about Quine's arguments against essentialism. In the first place, Quine has attempted to show that essentialism (of the second and the third grade) is a bewildering and paradoxical notion. These attempts, it seems to me, have been adequately refuted by Marcus (1967) and Cartwright (1968), so I will not discuss them further. Second, Quine has objected that essentialism is inconsistent with the attempt to explain necessity via analyticity. He says in his essay "Reference and Modality,"

> Essentialism is abruptly at variance with the idea favoured by Carnap, Lewis, and others, of explaining necessity by analyticity. For the appeal to analyticity can pretend to distinguish essential and accidental traits of an object only relative to how the object is specified, not absolutely ((1961) p. 155).

Gibbard (1975) has claimed that this is not so—that one can explain necessity via analyticity and yet embrace essentialism for individual concepts. Further, several philosophers, notably Plantinga, have attempted to explain modality *de re* in terms of modality *de dicto*. If these attempts are successful, it would appear that even essentialism for ordinary objects is no more a problem for Carnap and Lewis than is *de dicto* necessity. I will not, however, pursue the point, believing as I do, that even necessity *de dicto* cannot be explained in terms of analyticity (see pp. 128–29 of this book; see also Thomason (1976).)

A third set of Quinean qualms center on trans-world identity. If it makes sense to say of *this man* that he is essentially rational, then it must make sense to identify the same man across possible worlds. But identifying individuals across worlds, according to Quine, is an idea with dubious meaning. In a recent paper (1976) he contrasts our methods of identifying an object from moment to moment with the method (or lack thereof) of identifying an object from world to world.

> [O]ur cross-moment identifications of bodies turned on continuity of displacement, distortion, and chemical change. These considerations can not be extended across worlds, because you can change anything to anything by easy stages through some connecting series of possible worlds ((1976) p. 861).

This point is reminiscent of Chisholm's contention that by gradually and appropriately changing Adam's and Noah's properties through a series of worlds we can arrive at a world in which Adam and Noah have, so to speak, switched identities. The bulk of this section is devoted to an attempt to answer this charge. But before we see how Chisholm (and Quine) can be answered, it is best to develop Chisholm's argument in some detail. In the following presentation I have changed Chisholm's example, but the substance of his argument remains. Instead of Adam and Noah interchanging their identities, two bicycles, Charlie and Alfred, after suffering small changes through a series of possible worlds, will switch identities. I believe that this change of example makes Chisholm's argument more persuasive. (I have benefitted in my presentation of Chisholm's problem from reading Chandler (1976).)

Let me begin by making explicit some of the intuitions on which the following argument will rest.

The first intuition. A bicycle that comes into existence made up of some parts $P_1, \ldots, P_n$ could have come into existence with any *one* of its parts different.

The second intuition. A bicycle that comes into existence at a place p and at a time t could have come into existence at a slightly different place p′ and at a slightly different time t′.

Some doubts may be raised about the validity of the first intuition. It may be argued that a bicycle could have had some of its parts different (at the point of origin)—for example, it could have had a different spoke or a different washer—but that some parts of the bicycle could not have been different. For example, it could not have come into existence with a different frame. This I think is correct, given the way bicycles are actually constructed. But suppose for the purposes of the argument that even grosser parts of bicycles are assemblies of numerous small parts. Under this supposition I think we can agree that the first intuition holds. (We can construct a more elaborate version of the argument without this supposition. But let us keep things simple.) Note that both intuitions are understood to apply not only to the actual bicycles but also to "possible" bicycles. If a bicycle comes into existence made up of $P_1, \ldots, P_n$ in the world w, then it is possible that it might have come into existence made up of Q, $P_2, \ldots\ldots, P_{n-1}$, and it is also possible that it might have come into existence at a slightly different place and at a slightly different time.

Now suppose that two bicycles, Charlie and Alfred, come into existence in the actual world made up of $P_1, \ldots, P_n$ and $Q_1, \ldots, Q_n$, respectively. We suppose that *n* is very large, that Charlie and Alfred are assemblies of a very large number of small parts. We also suppose that all the "corresponding" parts of Charlie and Alfred are interchangeable. That is, bicycles could have been made of $P_1, \ldots, P_{i-1}$, $Q_i, \ldots, P_n$ and $Q_1, \ldots, Q_{i-1}, P_i, \ldots, Q_n$. Now our intuitions are that Charlie and Alfred could have had one part different, and more particularly that Charlie and Alfred could have come into existence with any one part interchanged.[4] Thus we intuit that there is a world W′ where Charlie comes into existence made up of Q_1, $P_2, \ldots, P_n$, and Alfred comes into existence made up of $P_1, Q_2, \ldots, Q_n$. But now consider Charlie and Alfred in W′. Here, too, we intuit that they could

4. I do not mean to suggest that the first intuition *logically implies* that Charlie and Alfred could come into existence with any one part interchanged. This latter claim is a plausible extension of our first intuition and indeed is implied by it under certain very plausible assumptions.

have come into existence with any one part interchanged. Thus there is a world W″, where Charlie and Alfred come into being as assemblies of $Q_1, Q_2, P_3, \ldots, P_n$ and $P_1, P_2, Q_3, \ldots, Q_n$, respectively. By reasoning similarly, we arrive at a world W*, where Charlie and Alfred have interchanged all their parts. In W* Charlie is made up of $Q_1, \ldots, Q_n$, and Alfred of $P_1, \ldots, P_n$. Finally, by gradually varying their place and time of origin, we arrive at a world W, where Charlie and Alfred interchange their point of origin. Charlie in W comes into existence at the place and time where Alfred actually comes into existence, and, similarly, Alfred in W comes into existence at the place and time where Charlie actually comes into existence. Thus in W it appears that Charlie and Alfred have interchanged all their actual properties: they have interchanged all their parts, and they have also interchanged their point of origin.

A simpler version of this argument is illustrated below (see figure 2). Here Charlie and Alfred are made up of P_1, P_2, P_3 and Q_1, Q_2, Q_3, respectively, in the actual world W_1. Via a number of "easy stages" we arrive at the world W_4, where they have interchanged all their parts. And finally in W_5, Alfred and Charlie interchange their point of origin. There is some fudge here in the last step. This can be removed as follows. Suppose that in W_1 some workman assembles Charlie and Alfred thus. He picks up P_1 from the bicycle parts P_1–P_3 and Q_1–Q_3 that lie scattered on his workbench, and he puts it on the left (see figure 2); then he places Q_1 on the right, and then P_2 on the left. He continues this way until the assembly of Charlie and Alfred (i.e., L_1 and R_1) is complete. World W_2 is exactly like W_1 except that here the workman assembles the parts in the order Q_1–P_1–P_2–Q_2–P_3–Q_3, creating assemblies L_2 and R_2. And similarly for the other worlds W_3 to W_5. Now if we contemplate the transitions from W_1 to W_2, and from W_2 to W_3, etc., I think we are forced to conclude that Charlie and Alfred "survive" the small changes. In particular, identity is preserved in the transition from W_4 to W_5. Charlie in W_4 (i.e., L_4) is the same bicycle as R_5 in W_5. R_5 comes into being slightly later than L_4, and its place of origin is slightly to the right of L_4; but aside from this, R_5 is exactly like L_4. So, by the second intuition, we judge that R_5 is the same bicycle as L_4. Similarly, we conclude that Alfred in W_4 (i.e., R_4) is the same bicycle as L_5. Note that Charlie of W_5 has the place

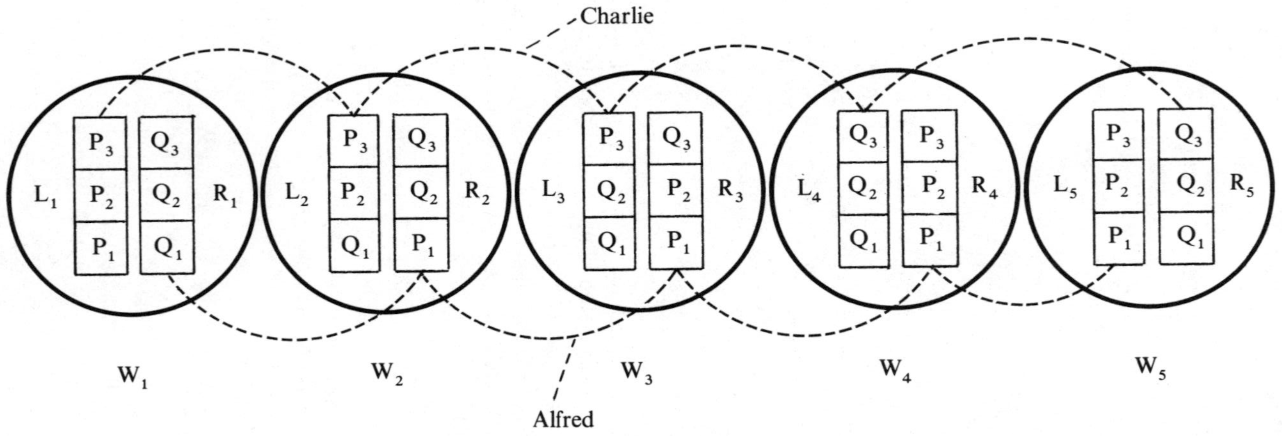

(i) W_1–W_5 are five possible worlds.
(ii) P_1, P_2, P_3, Q_1, Q_2, Q_3 are parts from which two bicycles, Charlie and Alfred, are made.
(iii) L_n and R_n are, respectively, the left and the right bicycles displayed in W_n ($1 \leq n \leq 5$).
(iv) The dashed lines indicate the trans-world identifications of Charlie and Alfred.

Figure 2

and time of origin of Alfred of W_1; and Alfred of W_5 has the place and time of origin of Charlie of W_1.

Our first two intuitions dictate that identities (22)–(25) hold:

(22) L_1 is the same bicyclc as L_2,

(23) L_2 is the same bicycle as L_3,

(24) L_3 is the same bicycle as L_4,

(25) L_4 is the same bicycle as R_5.

These yield by transitivity of identity that L_1 is the same bicycle as R_5. Now this is a difficult conclusion to accept. For, intuitively, we do not think it possible that a bicycle could have come into existence with all its parts as well as its place and time of origin different. The first and the second intuitions, on the assumption of trans-world identity, conflict with this third intuition.

The third intuition. A bicycle that comes into existence made up of parts $P_1, \ldots, P_n$ at a place p and time t could not have come into existence made up of entirely different parts and at a different place p′ and a different time t′.

Furthermore, worlds such as W_5 are very paradoxical. *Prima facie*, W_5 is distinct from W_1; Charlie in W_1 is made up of P_1, P_2, and P_3, but in W_5, Charlie is made up of Q_1, Q_2, and Q_3. Yet there does not seem to be a real difference between these worlds. By hypothesis they are the same except in the way our workman assembles the two bicycles. But in this respect, too, nothing distinguishes them. The workman assembles the same parts in the same order at the same time in W_1 and W_5. The order of assembly in both worlds is P_1–Q_1–P_2–Q_2–P_3–Q_3. What discernible difference is there between W_1 and W_5? As Chisholm asks, "Could God possibly have had a sufficient reason for creating [W_1] instead of [W_5]?"

Several ways of solving this problem are suggested in the literature. I examine them briefly before presenting my own solution.

Chisholm's solution of the problem employs "individual essences." The idea is that for each object d (or better each *K*) there are certain properties E (called the "individual essence of d") which individuate it in a very strong way. The object d has E in all the worlds in which it exists, and any object that possesses E in any world is identical to d. That is, at all worlds w, d and only d has the properties E. Trivial individuating properties, such as "being identical to Charlie" or "being assembled in such and such a place and such and such a time *in the actual world*," are excluded from E.

If objects have individual essences, then we can rule out strange worlds like W_5. In this purported world, Charlie and Alfred have interchanged all their properties and hence they have interchanged their essences—which by definition is impossible. We can say that somewhere in the sequence W_1 to W_5 we passed from the realm of possibility to the realm of impossibility. For somewhere along the line Charlie and Alfred lost their individual essences.

To make this solution really convincing we need to say more about *what* the individual essences of objects such as Charlie and Alfred are. It is insufficient to say that Charlie and Alfred have some individual essences without any further specification. The fact that nontrivial individual essences of objects are difficult to specify makes Chisholm's solution less than satisfying. Further, it appears that the doctrine of individual essences conflicts with our earlier intuitions—that a bicycle could have come into existence with any one part different and that it could have come into existence at a slightly different place and time. On the basis of these intuitions and certain logical properties of identity, we showed that Charlie and Alfred could interchange all their properties. Thus if we admit individual essences, it seems that we will have to reject some of our earlier intuitions. This is unsatisfactory because something more intuitive is given up in favor of something less intuitive, namely, individual essences.[5]

Another solution, a rather ingenious one, is offered by Chandler (1976). Chandler accepts the paradoxical conclusions of Chisholm's argument—that W_1 is distinct from W_5 and that L_1 is the same bicycle as R_5—but he shows that this is not inconsistent with our intuitions about possibility and necessity. For this purpose Chandler employs the accessibility relation between worlds. Possibility (and impossibility) according to Chandler is not an absolute property of worlds; worlds are possible only relative to other worlds. So, for example, W_2 and (perhaps) W_3 are "accessible" from W_1; that is, these worlds are

5. I should remark in fairness to Chisholm that he offers this solution in the context of his example of Adam and Noah's interchanging identities. In this case, it is more plausible to postulate individual essences, and to deny "intuitions" corresponding to our intuitions about bicycles.

possible relative to W_1. But W_5 is not possible relative to W_1. (It may, however, be possible relative to W_3. Accessibility is not required to be transitive.) Further, to evaluate a claim such as

Possibly x is thus and so

at a world w, we see if there is a world *possible relative to w* where x is thus and so. Now we can see how Chandler reconciles our three earlier intuitions concerning bicycles. Relative to W_1, there are worlds such as W_2 where Charlie and Alfred interchange any one part. Also, there are worlds accessible from W_1 where they interchange their point of origin. So the first two intuitions hold. Now Chisholm's argument shows on the basis of these intuitions that there are worlds like W_5 where Charlie and Alfred interchange all their properties. Chandler accepts the *existence* of these worlds but denies that they are accessible from W_1. Relative to W_1 there are no *accessible* worlds where Charlie and Alfred interchange all their parts and their point of origin. Hence the third intuition also holds. Chandler manages to preserve our intuitions and the transitivity of identity by giving up the transitivity of the accessibility relation. (It may be worth remarking that the accessibility relation, on its present interpretation, should be required to be reflexive and symmetric. This confirms a suspicion that many of us have harbored—that the *Brouwersche* system is *the* correct system of modal logic!)

Chandler's solution is clever, but it comes at a high price. Chandler is forced to say that W_1 and W_5 are numerically distinct worlds though they are identical in all respects (save the accessibility relations). This makes possible worlds very mysterious indeed. For each world there are infinitely many distinct worlds, exactly like it in all respects, but inaccessible from it. The mystery is deepened by the fact that the accessibility relations have no independent motivation.

Lewis (1968) would reject all this obscure metaphysical talk as arising from taking *identity* across worlds too seriously. Strictly speaking, Lewis would say, objects in different worlds are not identical. Objects of one world do not exist in other worlds. They have *counterparts* in other worlds. And these we identify, in loose talk, with the objects themselves. Thus, in our example, L_1 is a counterpart of L_2, and L_2 is a counterpart of L_3, and L_3 of L_4. But these objects are not identical in the strict sense as is shown by the fact that L_1 is not a counterpart of L_4. Lewis, I think, would accept Chisholm's argument as valid, but he would deny the paradoxical conclusion by denying one of the (implicit) premises: the transitivity of identity (or the counterpart relation).

When I first thought about Chisholm's problem, I felt that its source was the vagueness in the principles of identity. It seemed to me that in Chisholm's example, as in other paradoxes due to vagueness, such as the Bald Man and the Sorites, a large number of small differences add up to a big difference. As we move from one world to another, from W_1 to W_2 and W_2 to W_3 and so on, our intuition is that the differences are small and that the identity is preserved. But when we consider a large sequence of these changes together, W_1 to W_5, our intuition is that the identity is lost. This situation seemed to me to be parallel to the Bald Man. The bald man grows one hair; he remains bald. He grows one more and is still bald. And one more. After a large number of these small changes, we intuit that the man is not bald; but paradoxically our reasoning leads to a contrary conclusion.

As I said, my first reaction to Chisholm's problem was that it was caused by vagueness. But I did not know how the paradox could be explained within a systematic theory. I did not know how vagueness in identity could be represented and understood. However, once I learned how principles of identity of common nouns are represented in modal logics, it seemed to me that a solution of the problem was at hand. We know that common nouns express sorts and that sorts can be thought of as collections of principles of identity (ignoring non-substance nouns). These principles of identity trace *particulars*—a particular man, or bicycle, or whatever—through worlds (and times). Now we can allow these principles to be vague. A vague principle of identity for a particular, say, this bicycle, may yield two values at some world. This is understood to mean that the principle of identity leaves undetermined which of the two values is the same bicycle as our original. A vague common noun such as 'bicycle' expresses a *vague sort*, which is roughly a collection of vague principles of identity (for particulars). A logic of vague sorts, I thought, would not be too difficult to develop. We simply employ something like van Fraassen's super-valuation technique.

It seemed to me a considerable merit of our theory of common nouns that it could be generalized to take into account vagueness in the principles of identity. But I soon came to see that Chisholm's problem had nothing to do with vagueness. This I think can be readily proved. It is a mark of paradoxes which rely on vagueness that they dissolve once the vagueness is arbitrarily removed. Thus consider the Bald Man again.

Premise. A man with no hair (or 0 hair) is bald.

Premise. For any n, if a man with n hairs is bald, then a man with $n + 1$ hairs is bald.

Conclusion. For every number n, a man with n hairs is bald.

In this argument, if we arbitrarily remove vagueness from the predicate 'bald'—say we stipulate that a man with 10^6 or more hairs is not bald, but a man with fewer hairs is bald—then the argument ceases to be paradoxical. The second premise is now readily seen to be false. Chisholm's argument, however, does not have this character. The paradox remains even when the vagueness is arbitrarily removed. Let us say that Charlie and Alfred can at most interchange the place and time of origin or just one part (but not both). Now according to this (partial) rule of identity, (26)–(28) hold:

(26) L_1 is the same bicycle as L_2,

(27) L_2 is the same bicycle as L_3,

(28) L_3 is the same bicycle as L_4.

Also, (29) and (30) do not hold:

(29) L_1 is the same bicycle as L_3,

(30) L_1 is the same bicycle as L_4.

This conflicts with the transitivity of identity. And Chisholm's paradox remains. Vagueness is not responsible for this mischief!

The conclusion I now draw from Chisholm's argument is that our theory of common nouns is wrong, or at least that it is not general enough. Transitivity of identity is not the only assumption that is operative in Chisholm's argument; near separation of sorts (see chapter 3) is also tacitly employed. I suggest that we can solve the paradox and preserve the transitivity of identity if we weaken the requirement of near separation. Let me first explain how I propose to generalize the theory of common nouns. Then I will explain briefly how Chisholm's paradox can be explained away in the new theory.

(I should emphasize that what follows is a *brief* and *sketchy* presentation of the idea. I leave a more detailed exposition and defense for a later work.)

I propose that the requirement of near separation be weakened to *quasi-separation*. Let $\mathfrak{A} = \langle W, D, i^* \rangle$ be a model structure.

Definition 1. An intensional property $\mathscr{I}$ in $\mathfrak{A}$ is *nearly separated in* w iff all individual concepts i,i′ that belong to $\mathscr{I}$ at w are such that if $i(w_1) = i'(w_1) \neq i^*(w_1)$ at any world w_1, then $i = i'$.

Definition 2. An intensional property $\mathscr{I}$ in $\mathfrak{A}$ is *quasi-separated* iff $\mathscr{I}$ is nearly separated in every world.

Definition 3. A *quasi-sort* in $\mathfrak{A}$ is a quasi-separated intensional property.[6]

Common nouns in the new logic, L_5, are assigned quasi-sorts. Otherwise, the definitions of model, assignment, satisfaction, and truth are the same as for L_4 (see Definitions 11–13, chapter 3). Note that for L_5 the axiom schema AS13* is further weakened to

$$AS13^{**} \quad K[t_1] \wedge K[t_2] \supset . t_1 = t_2 \supset . \\ t_2 \neq \text{ገ}(K', y) y \neq y \supset \Box t_1 = t_2 .$$

The remaining axiom schemata of chapter 2 are valid for L_5. I conjecture that with AS13** they constitute a complete calculus for L_5.

The technical modifications I have proposed are relatively minor, but they cause major changes in our conception of trans-world identity. In the present proposal claims of trans-world identity must be relativized to a world. We should not say, for example, that

(31) R_2 is the same bicycle as R_3

holds absolutely, for this identity claim may be true relative to one world but false relative to another. Statements such as (31) need to be completed by a world parameter in the manner of (32); as they stand, they are incomplete.

(32) R_2 is the same bicycle as R_3 relative to W.

The connection between relativized identities and quasi-sorts is this.

Proposition 1. Let the common noun K express the quasi-sort $\mathscr{S}$ and let the individual concept i belong to $\mathscr{S}$ at w. Then ignoring

6. It is reasonable to put the following additional requirement on quasi-sorts. If $\mathscr{S}$ is a quasi-sort and the individual concepts i,i′ belong to $\mathscr{S}$ at w,w′, respectively, then $i(w') = i'(w')$ if $i(w) = i'(w)$.

considerations pertaining to existence, i(w) is a K in w and for any worlds w′, w″, i(w′) in w′ is the same [K] as i(w″) in w″ *from the point of view of* w.

The intension of a common noun K yields at each world w a set of individual concepts, and these concepts determine trans-world identities of K's from the point of view of w. As an illustration, consider the intension of 'bicycle' in our hypothetical example above. We suppose that vagueness in the principle of identity has been removed as before: we allow bicycles to interchange just one part or their point of origin but not both. Now the intension of 'bicycle' is represented by $\mathscr{S}$ displayed below. (In the following diagram * is the "nonexisting" individual. Note that only four worlds are displayed because in our view W_1 and W_5 turn out to be identical.)

$\mathscr{S}$:	W_1	W_2	W_3	W_4
	$L_1L_2{*}R_4$	$L_1L_2L_3{*}$	${*}L_2L_3L_4$	$L_1{*}R_3R_4$
	$R_1R_2{*}L_4$	$R_1R_2R_3{*}$	${*}R_2R_3R_4$	$R_1{*}L_3L_4$

The individual concepts falling under a world in $\mathscr{S}$ determine the trans-world identities of bicycles *relative to that world*. Thus, relative to W_1, L_1, L_2, and R_4 constitute the same bicycle. But relative to W_2 this is not so; here L_1, L_2, and L_3 constitute the same bicycle. It is the peculiar "indexical" nature of the principle of identity that motivates this relativity of identity and the weaker requirement on common nouns. The trans-world identities of a bicycle depend upon the bicycle's contingent properties (e.g., its parts at the origin). Hence what trans-world identities obtain depend upon the world we take as our reference point. Thus, relative to W_1, when we hold L_1 fixed, the principle of identity yields L_2 and R_4 as its bicycle "counterparts"; but when we hold the same bicycle fixed relative to W_2, we get L_1 and L_3 as its counterparts. By weakening the requirement on the intension of common nouns, we gain flexibility. We are able to represent principles of identity such as the one for 'bicycle'. Observe that the intensional property $\mathscr{S}$ is quasi-separated; it is not, however, nearly separated.

Relative identity is an equivalence relation. That is, the binary relation defined by

——— is the same [K] as ----- from the point of view of w

is weakly reflexive, symmetric, and transitive (see p. 36). This follows from the quasi-separation of the intension of *K*. But the relation of absolute identity defined by

(33) There is a world w such that ——— is the same [K] as ----- from the point of view of w

is *not* an equivalence relation. This relation, which is essentially the identity relation discussed in chapters 1 and 3, is an equivalence only if we suppose the intension of *K* to be separated (again ignoring existence).

Now we can see where the fallacious step lies in Chisholm's argument. We were persuaded that certain identities hold—namely, those claimed in (26)–(28). These seemed to imply by the transitivity of identity that L_1 is the same bicycle as L_4, which conflicts with the principle of identity for bicycles. We notice, though, that the transitivity of identity can only be supposed within a point of view, and claims (26)–(28) do not hold within *any* point of view. With W_1 as our vantage point, (27) fails to hold; relative to W_2, (28) fails; and so on. That is, (26)–(28) can be true together only if they are understood as involving different points of view. But so understood there is no reason to expect transitivity. The implicit assumption which leads us to expect transitivity here, and which makes Chisholm's argument so persuasive in the first place, is that identity is absolute—that it does not need to be relativized to a world. This assumption is none other than the assumption of the near separation of common nouns. By giving it up, we solve the paradox and preserve all the logical properties of identity.

The suggested solution has several merits. First, in our solution the worlds W_1 and W_5 are identical. The argument that "proved" otherwise is easily refuted. The alleged nonidentity of W_1 and W_5 was established on the basis of the claim that Charlie in W_1 (i.e., L_1) is made of P_1, P_2, P_3 in W_1, but the same bicycle in W_5 (R_5) is made of Q_1, Q_2, Q_3. This claim, however, is clearly false. L_1 and R_5 do not constitute the same bicycle from any point of view. The argument that they do, we have already seen, rested on the false supposition that the intension of 'bicycle' is nearly separated.

Second, all three of our initial intuitions are preserved. Take any bicycle in any world. It is true of this bicycle that it could have come into existence in a slightly different place and time and that it could have come into existence with any one part different. This, however, does not conflict with the intuition that the bicycle could not have come into existence with all its parts replaced. The argument that these intuitions are inconsistent relied on the same false assumption—that the intension of 'bicycle' is nearly separated.

I remark that once we accept quasi-separation as the proper requirement on the intensions of common nouns, the requirement of near (modal) constancy is no longer appropriate for substance nouns. This should be replaced by quasi-constancy.

Definition 4. The intensional property $\mathscr{I}$ in $\mathfrak{A}$ is *quasi-constant* iff, for every world $w \in W$, if an individual concept $i \in \mathscr{I}(w)$ and $i(w) \neq i^*(w)$, then for every world w' such that $i(w') \neq i^*(w')$, there is an individual concept $i' \in \mathscr{I}(w')$ such that $i'(w') = i(w')$ and $i'(w) = i(w)$.

Note that in the presence of (near) separation, quasi-constancy implies (near) modal constancy.

Finally, it should be remarked that although our three intuitions establish pretty conclusively that the common noun 'bicycle' does not express a sort—but only a quasi-sort—we do not have the corresponding intuitions for many other common nouns (e.g., 'man', 'tree'). It seems to me that we have intuitions of this kind only for terms for artifacts and assemblies—but not for other nouns, especially not for natural kind terms. Thus I conjecture that the difference in the logic of natural kind terms and the logic of terms for artifacts is this: the intensions of the former are nearly separated, but the intensions of the latter are only quasi-separated.

5 Modal Logic and Truth

Having dealt with Quine's objection to modal logic in chapter 4, I now turn to the second major criticism of modal logic, raised by Davidson and by Wallace. They have claimed, to quote Wallace, "that modal predicate calculus does not present a reasonable standpoint from which to interpret a language" ((1970) p. 147). The aim of this chapter is to present and evaluate their argument for this claim. It will help to bear in mind the general form of their argument.

Premise (1): A logic adequate for the interpretation of language must have a certain formal property P.

Premise (2): Modal predicate calculus does not have the property P.

Conclusion: Modal predicate calculus is not adequate for the interpretation of language.[1]

I explain and justify the first premise in §1. The justification relies on a particular conception of semantics developed and argued by Davidson. I begin §1 with a brief exposition and motivation of Davidson's semantic program, and I show how the program yields the adequacy condition on logics formulated in premise (1). Section 2 is devoted to Wallace's argument for premise (2). I evaluate the arguments presented in the first two sections in §3. The evaluation requires us to distinguish two concepts of truth which seem to be of independent philosophical interest. The last two sections, 4 and 5, are more technical than the rest. Here I present homophonic truth theories (see below for explanation) for a simplified version of L_1 and for Bressanian modal logics.

This chapter (with a different §4) appeared, under the same title, in the *Journal of Philosophical Logic*, vol. 7, no. 4 (1978).

1. I have some qualms about attributing this argument to Davidson and Wallace. Neither of them states or argues explicitly for premise (1). Harman (1972), however, has argued for this premise in the context of a Davidsonian semantic theory. Perhaps the argument should be called "the Davidson–Wallace–Harman argument."

§1. Davidson's Semantic Program

Davidson has argued in a number of interesting and important papers that to interpret a language is to construct a theory of truth for it (Davidson (1967), (1970), (1973a), (1973b)). A theory of truth for a language L is a finite theory, formulated in a metalanguage ML, which satisfies Tarski's convention T. That is, a theory of truth for L implies all sentences of the form

(T) x is true (in L) if and only if p,

where 'x' is replaced by a canonical description (in ML) of a sentence of L and 'p' is replaced by its translation in ML. (Sentences of the form (T) will sometimes be called *T-sentences* (of L), and sometimes *T-biconditionals* (of L).)

Note that the finiteness requirement on a theory of truth is understood in a strong way: the finitely many axioms of a theory of truth are required to generate all the T-sentences *without the aid of any other nonlogical axioms.* This has the consequence, for example, that a theory of truth cannot employ all the axioms of Peano arithmetic. It can employ only a finite subset of them.

When the metalanguage contains the object language, the identity function constitutes an adequate translation scheme (for Davidsonian purposes). The theory that results is called a *homophonic* theory of truth. The condition on logics formulated in premise (1) is understood as follows: homophonic theories of truth are constructible in logics adequate for the interpretation of language. We shall return to this adequacy condition later.

Davidson's proposal is essentially a criterion for the evaluation of semantic theories. A semantic theory for a language L is adequate by Davidson's criterion if it is finite and if it entails all the T-sentences of L. Before we see the merits of the proposal, two preliminary remarks should be made. First, as it stands, the proposal is unsatisfactory for natural languages. The presence of indexicals, ambiguity, vagueness, and semantic paradoxes in natural languages makes the criterion, in its present formulation, unsuitable. Consider, for example, ambiguity. (This is an interesting feature of a language to be explained by its semantic theory, and thus not to be ignored.) Let S be an ambiguous sentence of L. Now there is a problem applying Davidson's criterion if the metalanguage does not contain the corresponding ambiguity:

what sentence of ML will replace '*p*' in the T-sentence for *S*? Even if the metalanguage contains the ambiguity, an equally difficult problem remains. Suppose, for concreteness, that the object language is a fragment of English, English*, and the metalanguage is English. The identity function now suffices for the translation of all sentences, ambiguous or otherwise. An adequate semantic theory, according to the criterion above, will yield T-sentences such as

(1) $\overline{\text{The president of the United States was a Democrat}}$ is true in English* iff the president of the United States was a Democrat.

($\ulcorner \bar{\alpha} \urcorner$ represents a structural descriptive name of α.)

Now, as a sentence of English, (1) is ambiguous and it has two readings. And the semantic theory can be understood as asserting (1) on just one of these readings or on both these readings. If the former, then the theory does not take into account the ambiguity of 'the president of the United States was a Democrat'. If the latter, then at least one reading of (1) is false (in December 1976). In either case the semantic theory that entails (1) is unacceptable. This shows that the criterion formulated above needs revision to deal with ambiguity. Davidson has suggested several ways of modifying the criterion to make it adequate for natural languages. It cannot be said that he has succeeded in this task entirely. (His latest proposal to deal with ambiguity, in Davidson (1970), is in my opinion unsatisfactory.) However, since natural languages are not the focus of this discussion, I shall suppose that the criterion can, with appropriate modifications, serve for natural languages.

My second preliminary remark is this. The characterization above of a theory of truth is not quite true to Davidson. Davidson's requirements on a theory of truth are weaker. *A Davidsonian theory of truth is not required to fulfill Tarski's convention T*. Davidson requires that a theory of truth for a language L (in ML) must imply for each object language sentence *x*, a sentence of the form

(D) *x* is true (in L) if and only if *p*,

where '*p*' is replaced by a sentence of the metalanguage which has the same truth value as *x*. *It is not required that p be a translation in ML of x.* The only requirement that is put on the biconditionals is that they be true. Davidson has argued that a theory of language which meets these minimal requirements deserves to be called a theory of meaning. He has argued that (1) such a theory shows how the meaning of a sentence depends upon the meanings of its parts, (2) it gives the meaning of each sentence of the object language, and (3) it is empirically testable. If the second claim is right, then a Davidsonian truth theory will satisfy convention T. However, the point to be noted is that this is no simple consequence of the definition of a theory of truth; it requires an extended philosophical argument. I now discuss these claims.

A theory of truth shows how the meaning of a sentence depends upon the meanings of its parts. Since a theory of truth is required to be finite and since it must account for an infinity of biconditionals, it will of necessity work in a recursive way. A theory of truth will analyze each sentence in terms of a finite number of truth-relevant *basic expressions* and in terms of a finite number of truth-affecting *constructions*. It will give outright the semantic properties of the basic expressions, and it will show how the constructions affect the semantic properties of the expressions on which they operate. Thus a theory of truth will show how the semantic properties of wholes depend upon the semantic properties of their parts (Davidson (1973a)).

A theory of truth gives the meaning of each sentence of the object language. This point reinforces the previous one. If a theory of truth gives the *meaning* of the object language sentences, then it is plausible to say that it also shows how the meaning of a sentence depends upon the meanings of words. This is so because the theory, working in a recursive manner, gives the meaning of all the sentences on the basis of the semantic properties of a finite number of basic expressions.

A theory that satisfies convention T automatically gives the meaning of each object language sentence. For such a theory implies all the T-sentences of the object language, and T-sentences by definition correlate object language sentences with their metalanguage translations. But, as we noted above, a Davidsonian theory is not required to meet convention T; here the translation requirement is dropped from the biconditionals. By Davidson's criterion, a theory that implies

(2) 'Snow is white' is true (in English) iff grass is green

is no less acceptable than ones that imply

(3) 'Snow is white' is true (in English) iff snow is white.

What considerations preclude the theories that imply (2)? What reason is there to suppose that a Davidsonian truth theory will invariably "correlate" object language sentences with their metalanguage translations?

The answer lies in the holistic constraint on a theory of truth. A theory of truth is required to generate, for *each* sentence of the object language, a biconditional of the form (D). It must pair each object language sentence with a metalanguage sentence of the same truth value. It is not easy to see how a theory that meets this constraint could reasonably generate (2). Since 'is white' occurs in an infinity of sentences (and it is a "meaningful unit"), the truth theory will correlate it to a metalanguage predicate. This cannot be 'is green' because this will violate Davidson's requirement; now some true object language sentence will be correlated to a false metalanguage sentence. We can, of course, construct *ad hoc* theories that imply (2). For example, we may add (2) as an additional axiom to an otherwise acceptable truth theory for English. But this does not argue against the present point: that reasonable (and hence non–*ad hoc*) truth theories always pair sentences with their translations.

It may be argued, however, that the holistic constraint, though it precludes *arbitrary* correlation of true (false) object language sentences with true (false) metalanguage sentences, yet it does not yield anything like meaning. For, consider a theory for a language L couched in a first order extensional metalanguage. The theory will give outright the satisfaction conditions for atomic sentences, and it will also give clauses which show how the satisfaction conditions of wholes depend upon the satisfaction conditions of their parts; that is, it will have a number of basis clauses and a number of recursive clauses. For example, one of the basis clauses in a theory of English may be

(4) The object d satisfies *x* is a creature with a heart iff d is a creature with a heart.[2]

The point to note is that we may replace the predicate in the right-hand side of a basis clause by any other that is coextensive without

2. I have omitted reference to sequences for simplicity. Also, it is unlikely that a *good* theory of truth will treat 'is a creature with a heart' as an unanalyzed basic expression. Anyhow, let us go along with this clause for illustration purposes.

violating Davidson's criterion. The theory will still correlate truths with truths and falsehoods with falsehoods. In (4), for instance, we may replace 'creature with a heart' by 'creature with a kidney' on the right-hand side, and the theory will not imply any false biconditionals. Thus it seems that a theory that meets Davidson's criterion need not correlate an object language sentence with its metalanguage translation; at best, the correlation yields extensional isomorphism.

I do not know what Davidson would say to this[3]; perhaps he would retreat to Quine's thesis of the indeterminacy of translation and meaning (which he cites favorably). But it is open to him to say (though he would not say it) that the above argument shows that extensional logics are poor vehicles for the interpretation of language! Intensional logics are better suited for this purpose. Truth theories constructed in modal logics yield finer distinctions of meaning—in fact, up to intensional isomorphism.[4]

A theory of truth is empirically testable. It is this aspect of a theory of truth that distinguishes Davidson's approach from its main rival: the model-theoretic approach to semantics. Both Davidsonian ("truth-theoretic") semantics and model-theoretic semantics are empirical in the broad sense. Both sorts of semantics, for example, validate certain arguments; they classify certain sentences as logically (or analytically) true; and so on. And these consequences can be verified by comparison with the relevant *intuitions.* The difference between the two is that while a model-theoretic semantics can be verified *only* by reference to such intuitions, a truth-theoretic semantics can be verified in other ways. We can verify a Davidsonian semantics by verifying the biconditionals it implies. This evidently does not rely on intuitions

3. Davidson (1973b) seems to weaken the claim that a theory of truth gives the meaning of the object language sentences. He says, "A T-sentence of an empirical theory of truth can be used to interpret a sentence...provided we also know that the T-sentence is entailed by some true theory that meets the formal *and empirical criteria*" (p. 326, italics mine). Now it appears that theories of truth give meaning only when they meet Davidson's empirical criteria. I do not think that this additional constraint helps him with the present difficulty.

4. I should remark that the concept of translation cannot, in any case, be defined within the truth theory. We need a theory of inference *for the metalanguage* to define the translation function. Thus translation can only be defined in the meta-metalanguage (which can be identical to the metalanguage if the latter can do its own syntax).

about validity, synonymy, and the like.[5] In fact, Davidson argues that very little understanding of the object language is required to confirm the biconditionals (and hence the theory). All we need is to locate the speaker's attitude of assent and dissent. If we can tell whether the speaker, when presented with a sentence, assents to it or dissents from it, we have enough to confirm (or disconfirm) the biconditionals and the theory. We test a biconditional,

x is true (in L) if and only if p,

by seeing if the speakers of L assent to x when and only when p. (The method is a bit more complicated than this, but the idea should be clear. See Davidson (1973b) for a more accurate account.) This procedure requires us to suppose that the sentences a speaker assents to are true and the ones he dissents from are false. The supposition, Davidson argues, is a justified one (at least as a first step). He says that "disagreement and agreement alike are intelligible only against a background of massive agreement" (Davidson (1973b) p. 324).

Truth-theoretic semantics, then, can be tested without reliance on "linguistic intuitions." This is an important point in their favor. For one thing, the status of intuitions is not completely clear. What reason is there to suppose that a theory which accounts for "linguistic intuitions" has anything to do with language, rather than with a curious psychological phenomenon? Also if, as some philosophers have argued, concepts such as synonymy and analyticity are suspect, then intuitions about them are doubly suspect. Truth-theoretic semantics have the virtue that they can be confirmed (infirmed) by evidence which is more readily available and which is not similarly suspect.

A further related point is this. Linguistic intuitions, on which model-theoretic semantics rely, are available only to the native speakers of the language. Hence we can construct model-theoretic semantics for a language only after we have interpreted and understood the language well enough to have the relevant intuitions (or we have managed to gain access to those intuitions in some indirect way, e.g., through some shared language). But truth-theoretic semantics can be verified by the sort of evidence that is available to a foreign speaker. Hence,

5. This is one of the motivations for dropping the translation requirement from the T-biconditionals.

Davidson argues, they give us a deeper understanding of language. Truth-theoretic semantics answer a good question: how is radical translation (or as Davidson prefers to call it "radical interpretation") possible? (I will not here describe the exact role of truth theory in radical interpretation. The reader is referred to Davidson (1973b).)

Davidson's conception of semantics leads naturally to the condition on logics formulated earlier: a logic is adequate for interpretation only if homophonic theories of truth can be constructed in it. I should emphasize at the outset that this is not an *absolute* adequacy condition on logics. The condition says only that to be suitable for a certain purpose, namely, interpretation of language, a logic must have a certain property. A logic may be unsuitable for this particular purpose but may be admirably suited for many others (e.g., formalization of science). Semantics of languages is one of the important applications of logics, but it is not the only one.

The role of logics in semantic interpretation is twofold. First, a logic provides logical (or semantic) structures for the object language sentences. It views sentences of the object language as built up of a number of basic expressions and a number of logical constants. Second, a logic is used to *interpret* the logical structures and hence the object language. That is, a logic is used to give a theory of truth for the logical structures. This yields a theory of truth for the object language.

The adequacy condition on logics says that a logic suitable for the first role is suitable for the second role. A logic in which homophonic truth theories cannot be constructed, one that is unsuitable for the second role, is unsuitable for the first role too. To see the plausibility of this, suppose that we use an intensional logic to provide the "logical forms" of the object language sentences. Also, suppose that we cannot use this logic for interpretation. We use instead, say, first-order extensional logic. Now we will have two logical forms associated with the object language sentences: one by the intermediary intensional logic and the other by the extensional logic. But it is clear that in a theory of this kind, the forms associated by the extensional language are basic. The logical forms imposed by the intensional logic seem useless intermediaries. As Harman (1972) complains about such theories, "... the logical forms assigned to sentences of the object language [by the intensional logic] are not taken seriously. They are not treated as semantically basic, since they are not used—only referred to—in giving the truth conditions of sentences."[6] If intensional logics have any claim to reveal logical form, they must not only be *interpretable* but they must do the *interpreting*. That is, homophonic truth theories must be available for them.

Davidson gives two additional arguments to show that extensional possible world semantics for intensional logics ("heterophonic truth theories") do not make them adequate for interpretation of languages. First, he points out that in these theories there is a large gap in the expressive resources of the object language and the metalanguage. There are sentences in the metalanguage with the same "subject matter" as the object language sentences but which cannot be translated in the object language, for example, 'a is F in exactly two worlds'. (See Hazen (1976) for a study of expressive incompleteness in modal logics.) The metalanguage in heterophonic truth theories is substantially richer than the object language. This violates one of the desiderata of the semantics of natural languages. We would ideally like to give a semantic theory for a natural language within itself. Of course, Tarski's work shows that this ideal cannot be fully attained, but we can still approximate it by keeping the differences between the object language and the metalanguage to a minimum. Homophonic truth theories narrow the gap between the object language and the metalanguage; heterophonic theories, generally speaking, widen the gap.

Davidson's second argument is that the heterophonic truth theories show intensionality to be a feature of the lack of expressive power.[7] He says,

> [T]he real contribution of extensional possible world semantics to the understanding of natural language may be to encourage us to see talk of necessity and the rest as intensional only when placed in a restricted setting; in the context of a fuller scheme, intensionality is revealed as a surface phenomenon. The underlying structure is extensional (Davidson (1973a) p. 83).

6. I have dropped the subscript 'm' from 'truth'. This does not change the sense of Harman's remark.

7. Davidson attributes this point to Wallace.

If we take seriously the universality of natural languages ("if we can speak meaningfully about anything at all, we can also speak about it in colloquial language"[8]), then this establishes that natural languages are not intensional. For intensionality is a mark of expressive incompleteness, and natural languages are expressively complete. It follows that modal logics do not reveal the logical forms of natural language sentences.

It is true that many modal logics are expressively incomplete relative to their extensional metalanguage. But this, it seems to me, does not establish that intensionality is the *result* of expressive incompleteness. There are modal logics that are expressively complete but where intensionality remains. In Bressanian modal logics, for example, we can "define" analogues of worlds (see §5), and, consequently, these are expressively complete. Further, even in standard modal logics we can trivially obtain expressive completeness by adding two predicates, 'is a world' and 'is instantiated' (and the corresponding axioms), *but this does not eliminate intensionality*. Hence intensionality is not an effect of expressive incompleteness. Davidson's second argument, therefore, fails. The first argument is somewhat more promising. It establishes that expressively incomplete modal logics are unsuitable for the interpretation of natural languages *if homophonic truth theories cannot be constructed in them*. For the gap in expressive power between the metalanguage and the object language results when one is taken to be extensional logic and the other modal logic. (Clearly, the argument does not touch expressively complete modal logics.)

§2. *Wallace's Argument*

Now I turn to the second premise: that homophonic theories of truth cannot be constructed in modal logics. John Wallace has argued that the most plausible strategy for constructing such theories fails. I present his argument in this section.

The main difficulty in constructing theories of truth in modal logics arises not in the quantificational part, nor in the interaction between quantification and modality, but rather in the clause for necessity. So, for simplicity, suppose that our object language (OL) is a modal *propositional* language, say with two atomic sentences p, q. Let our

8. Tarski (1956a), p. 164.

metalanguage (ML) be a quantified modal logic with atomic sentences p, q and with resources to form structural descriptive names of the object language expressions. Thus ML has something equivalent to Quine's corner quotes. Consider now how a homophonic truth theory for OL can be given in ML. We may, to begin with, adopt the following standard clauses for the nonmodal part. (Here and below the axioms of our theory are the universal closures of the displayed formulas.)

(5) $T(\ulcorner p \urcorner) \equiv p.$
(6) $T(\ulcorner q \urcorner) \equiv q.$
(7) $T(\ulcorner \sim X \urcorner) \equiv \sim T(X).$
(8) $T(\ulcorner (X \wedge Y) \urcorner) \equiv (T(X) \wedge T(Y)).$

'T' is the truth predicate for OL in ML, and 'X', 'Y' are variables of ML ranging over the object language sentences.

Axioms (5)–(8), when conjoined with the standard syntactic axioms, suffice to generate for each nonmodal sentence A of OL a biconditional of the form:

(H) $T(\bar{A}) \equiv A$ ($\bar{A}$ is a structural descriptive name for A.)

For the necessity clause,

(9) $T(\ulcorner \Box X \urcorner) \equiv \Box T(X)$

is a natural candidate. But this as yet does not help us to deduce all the instances of (H). For example, the theory does not imply

(10) $T(\overline{\Box p}) \equiv \Box p.$

This is so because axioms (5)–(8) do not entitle us to replace the left-hand side by the right-hand side in all contexts. They license the replacement only in the extensional contexts. Wallace points out that to overcome this and other similar difficulties we must strengthen (5)–(9) to their necessitations. Our axioms now are:

(11) $\Box(T(\ulcorner p \urcorner) \equiv p),$
(12) $\Box(T(\ulcorner q \urcorner) \equiv q),$
(13) $\Box(T(\ulcorner \sim X \urcorner) \equiv \sim T(X)),$
(14) $\Box(T(\ulcorner (X \wedge Y) \urcorner) \equiv (T(X) \wedge T(Y))),$
(15) $\Box(T(\ulcorner \Box X \urcorner) \equiv \Box T(X)).$

These would now imply all the instances of (H) provided our logic has the S4 axiom

$\Box A \supset \Box \Box A.$

In its absence we shall not be able to infer instances of (H) such as

$T(\overline{\Box\Box p}) \equiv \Box\Box p.$

For such logics it appears that an infinity of axioms is required to infer all instances of (H). Thus modal logics without the S4 axiom are subject to the argument that the requisite theory of truth cannot be constructed in a finite way.[9]

Wallace has argued that axioms (11)–(15) do not constitute an adequate truth theory even for modal logics with the S4 axiom. He points out that these axioms imply not only instances of the form (H) but also their necessitations:

(16) $\Box(T(\bar{A}) \equiv A)$.

These, Wallace argues, are false. Hence any theory that entails them is false too. Unfortunately, Wallace argues for the falsity of (16) only when $\Box$ is given the reading "It is logically necessary that." (This is unfortunate because on Wallace's reading quantified modal logics make sense only on the substitutional interpretation of quantifiers.) Wallace understands a sentence to be logically necessary if and only if it is true in virtue of its logical form—that is, if the sentence remains true under all reinterpretations of its nonlogical constants. He notes that an instance of (16),

(17) $\Box$($\overline{\text{Lizzy is playful}}$ is true (in English) ≡ Lizzy is playful),

is true on this reading of $\Box$ only if we regard all constants, '$\overline{\text{Lizzy is playful}}$', 'is true', 'Lizzy', and 'is playful', as logical constants. Besides being unreasonable, this move provides no help to modal logics. For now, all modal distinctions collapse. Logical necessity reduces to the extensional "It is true that."

Wallace does not *argue* for the falsity of (16) on the other readings of $\Box$. He says, however, that it is false "if '$\Box$' represents practically any other non-truth-functional sentential operator, e.g., 'Nikita believes

9. Of course if the logic has the thesis $\Box\Box A \supset \Box\Box\Box A$, then again a finite truth theory can be constructed. We simply take as our axioms the necessitations of (11)–(15). The claim footnoted is meant to apply to those logics which do not have even weaker versions of the S4 axiom. That is, no schemata of the form

$$\underbrace{\Box \ldots \Box}_{n\text{-times}} A \supset \underbrace{\Box\Box \ldots \Box}_{n+1\text{-times}} A$$

are valid.

that'" ((1970) p. 140). He adds in a later paper (Wallace (1975)) that (16) is false when □ is interpreted as physical necessity and tautologousness. It is curious that Wallace does not talk about the most familiar interpretation of □, namely, metaphysical necessity. It may be that Wallace thinks that this is a meaningless notion. In any case, since he holds that (16) is false when □ is read as physical necessity, he would also hold that it is false, if meaningful, when □ is read as metaphysical necessity.

Now why are instances of (16) false when □ is read as "It is physically necessary that" or as "It is metaphysically necessary that"? Presumably because of the possibility that words may change their meaning. Consider again (17). If 'Lizzy' in English had been used to talk about, say, Martha—the morose and unplayful child—then the sentence 'Lizzy is playful' would have been false—though, of course, this change of name would leave Lizzy's playfulness unaffected. That is, in a world w in which 'Lizzy' is used by English speakers as a name of Martha, but which otherwise is like our own, the antecedent

'Lizzy is playful' is true (in English)

is false (in the English of our world!), but the consequent

Lizzy is playful

is true. Hence the biconditional

'Lizzy is playful' is true (in English) ≡ Lizzy is playful

is false in w. Since w is conceivable, (17) is false when □ is read as metaphysical necessity. Also, w appears to be physically possible. It does not seem to be a law of nature, nor a consequence of one, that English speakers use 'Lizzy' to talk about Lizzy. (If we are tempted to say that it is, on the basis of some form of physical determinism, we should remember that it would not help the case for modal logic, for on this view modal distinctions collapse.) Hence (17) is false when □ is interpreted as physical necessity.

If the considerations above are right, they establish that (16) is false on many (perhaps all) familiar readings of □. Thus the most plausible strategy for constructing a homophonic truth theory in modal logics leads to a false and hence unreasonable theory.

§3. Two Concepts of Truth

To properly evaluate the above argument we should distinguish the following two concepts of truth. On the first concept (here represented by T_1 (= 'is-a-true$_1$-sentence-of-L')), a sentence A is true in a world w if and only if A is true in w *with the meaning it has* (*in* L) *in w*. On the second concept of truth (represented by T_2 (= 'is-a-true$_2$-sentence-of-L')), a sentence A is true in w if and only if A is true in w *with the meaning it has in the actual world.*

Truth as applied to sentences depends upon language and upon the world; it depends upon what a sentence means and upon what facts obtain in the world. To determine if A falls under the first concept of truth (T_1) in w, we take the meanings and the facts from w; but to determine if it falls under the second concept (T_2) in w, we take the meanings from the actual world and the facts from w. The two concepts can be explained in terms of the concept of "propositional truth":

> A belongs to the extension of T_1 at w iff there is a proposition p such that A expresses (in L) p in w and p is true in w.
>
> A belongs to the extension of T_2 at w iff there is a proposition p such that A expresses p in the actual world and p is true in w.

Both concepts of truth are present in our ordinary conceptual scheme. We can and do say such things as

(18) All contradictions are necessarily false,

(19) 'Snow is white or it is not white' is necessarily true (in English).

In one sense of these sentences (the sense in which they would most naturally be uttered and understood), they are true and they employ the second concept of truth. Statement (19), for example, says that the English sentence 'Snow is white or it is not white' is true in every world with the meaning it has in the actual world. We can represent (19) thus:

$\Box$(True$_2$-in-English ('Snow is white or it is not white')).

Clearly, (19), as well as (18), when understood in the most natural way, do not employ the first concept of truth (falsity).

In English we also say things which use the first concept. Compare

(20) If 'red' were to mean what 'white' means, then snow would be red,

(21) If 'red' were to mean what 'white' means, then 'Snow is red' would be true (in English).

These sentences say different things. (See Thomason (1976) for a theory that explains the difference.) Intuitively, we judge (21) to be true but (20) as false. If so, then 'true' in (21) must be understood as expressing the first concept of truth. If it expresses the second concept, (20) and (21) say the same thing, and hence they have the same truth value. A natural way to represent (21) is

(22) 'red' means what 'white' actually means $\mathrel{\overset{\Box}{\rightarrow}}$ True$_1$-in-English ('Snow is red').[10]

Now we can see how the Davidson–Wallace argument can be answered. First, if the condition on logics stated in premise (1) is understood to mean that homophonic theories of truth$_2$ can be constructed for adequate logics, it is clear that modal logics meet the condition *when* $\Box$ *is read either as physical necessity or as strict metaphysical necessity.* For with the second concept of truth the T-biconditionals

$$T_2(\bar{A}) \equiv A$$

are metaphysically necessary (and hence also physically necessary). Given our understanding of T_2, it is impossible to conceive a situation in which the two sides of the T-sentence have different truth values. Hence the most straightforward strategy (discussed in §2) succeeds in yielding a homophonic theory of truth$_2$ for modal logics. Axioms (11)–(15) constitute an adequate truth$_2$ theory for OL (§2). Wallace's objection is irrelevant because all it shows is that the biconditionals

$$T_1(\bar{A}) \equiv A,$$

employing the first concept, are not necessarily true.

Even if the adequacy condition is understood to require homophonic theories of truth$_1$, modal logics can meet it. We simply append to the theory of truth$_2$ the axiom

(23) $(\forall X)(T_2(X) \equiv T_1(X))$.[11]

Now the theory implies all the required biconditionals,

$$T_1(\bar{A}) \equiv A,$$

but it does not imply their necessitations. Wallace's objection again does not apply. We can grant that the sentences of the form

(24) $\Box(T_1(\bar{A}) \equiv A)$

are false, but this does not count against our theory. Note that we need a stronger version of (23), namely (25), to deduce instances of (24) (assuming the converse Barcan formula):

10. '$\mathrel{\overset{\Box}{\rightarrow}}$' is the counterfactual conditional (see Stalnaker (1968) and Lewis (1973)). I should note that (22) is not a completely accurate representation of (21). The inaccuracy is due to the occurrence of 'actually' in (22).

11. This important axiom is due to E. Schorsch.

(25) $\square(\forall X)(T_2(X) \equiv T_1(X))$,

which is clearly false. The extensions of T_2 and T_1 coincide at the actual world, but they do not coincide at all worlds.

We conclude, then, that homophonic theories of truth can be constructed for the modal logic OL (§2) when the $\square$ is interpreted as metaphysical (or as physical) necessity. There are no great difficulties in generalizing the method to quantified modal logics. Here, as usual, the theory of truth proceeds via the theory of satisfaction, and, for the most part, there are no difficulties with the latter. The standard techniques suffice for many systems of quantified modal logics, such as those of Thomason (1969). In modal logics with sortal quantification, a few new problems appear, but these can be solved using a theory of "modal" sequences. I give the theory in §4. For Bressanian logics, a nonstandard approach also succeeds in yielding homophonic truth theories. I give this approach in §5. The interest of the method lies in the fact that it can be used to give the definition of a more general concept of truth. (We can define something like the concept "the sentence x is true in the world w with the meaning it has in w′.") Also, truth theories in this method parallel the model theory more closely. Thus the method might be useful in giving theories of truth for weak modal systems, such as Von Wright's system M (Feys' T). As we noted above, axioms (11)–(15) do not imply the required T-sentences in weak modal logics. It appears that here an infinity of axioms are required in the truth theory. The strategy sketched in §5 may work for these weak systems. (This whole area requires more research. A particularly interesting question is that of a minimal modal logic: how weak can a quantified modal logic be and still meet the Davidsonian adequacy condition?) Despite the unfinished state of this inquiry, I think it is fair to conclude that many systems of quantified modal logic meet the adequacy condition. It is not surprising that some do not. If there weren't such systems, we would have to invent them!

What about the other readings of $\square$ mentioned by Wallace: logical necessity, belief, and tautologousness? With these interpretations, instances of (16) are false (or at least cannot be assumed to be true) even when 'T' represents the second concept of truth. Does Wallace's argument show that for these, at least, no intensional logic is possible?

I do not think so. All the argument shows is that the strategy sketched in §2 will not work for these readings of $\Box$. But even something as unsuitable for the "sentential-operator" interpretation as logical necessity can yield homophonic truth theories under the right conditions—for example, if we have quotation and quantification in and out of quotes (see Belnap and Grover (1973)). Here, of course, we can obtain truth theories trivially by an axiom such as

$$(\forall x)(T(`x') \equiv x).$$

If, however, quantification in and out is restricted to certain positions, say, to name and predicate positions (but not allowed in sentence positions), then we are forced to follow the recursive route.[12] And this route can be followed. All we need do is understand the logical constants of the metalanguage to include quotation, the truth predicate, and certain concepts of the morphology of the object language. Now adaptations of axioms (11)–(15) suffice. We have axioms such as

$$\Box(T(`x \wedge y') \equiv T(`x') \wedge T(`y')),$$
$$\Box(T(`\Box x') \equiv \Box T(`x')).$$

And these axioms, on our reading of $\Box$, are true. Note also that modal distinctions do not collapse.

Now I turn briefly to the first premise: that homophonic truth theories can be constructed in logics adequate for semantic interpretation. Does it formulate a reasonable adequacy condition on logics? I am skeptical. And this skepticism is rooted in my skepticism about Davidson's semantic program. *I am not convinced that Tarski's convention T (or Davidson's version of it) formulates a goal relevant to semantic theory.* The idea that it does rests on two claims which I find implausible. The first claim is that truth theories reveal something more about meanings than do model-theoretic semantics. With the latter, it appears that we learn only the recursive connection between the meanings of sentences and their parts; but with the former, it appears that we learn also the truth conditions, and hence the meanings, of the object language sentences. Thus truth theories seem to tell us not only *how* the meanings of wholes depend on the meanings of the parts but also *what* the meanings of the various wholes and parts are. I think

12. Thomason has observed that recursion is not forced on us if the object language and the metalanguage have complex predicates.

this is an illusion. Whatever we learn about meanings in a truth theory is revealed by the recursive clauses; the basis clauses, it seems to me, reveal nothing. The second claim is that model-theoretic semantics are empirically suspect (or at least that they do not provide an adequate methodological foundation for semantics). I think this is a fairly accurate criticism of the way model-theoretic semantics are usually presented: that is, as relying entirely on our linguistic intuitions about synonymy, analyticity, and the like. It seems to me, however, that a more adequate explanation is possible. We should see these semantics as relying not on intuitions about synonymy, etc., but rather on intuitions about more humdrum things—such as what kinds of answers are appropriate to such and such questions; what a speaker implies, insinuates, "implicates" by saying such and such in these contexts; and so on. The validity of these intuitions cannot be doubted. In fact, we can give a simple transcendental argument to show that for the most part these intuitions must be correct. We justify these intuitions by showing that if we were generally wrong about them, then the use of language would be impossible. In summary, then, I think that a more adequate methodological foundation can be provided for model-theoretic semantics if they are seen to be part of a broader theory of language.

These critical remarks against convention T are aimed only at Davidson's use of it: as a minimal requirement for theories of meaning. They do not apply to Tarski, who originally proposed the convention as the "material" adequacy condition for the definition of truth. Since there is much misunderstanding about Tarski's work on truth, I will comment briefly on it.

I think it is not much of an exaggeration to say that Davidson's and Tarski's aims are quite opposite. Whereas Davidson uses the concept of truth to explain intensional concepts such as meaning, Tarski's aim is to explain the concept of truth in terms of other concepts (possibly including intensional concepts). Just as in present-day philosophy there is skepticism about the meaningfulness and the empirical character of intensional concepts, in the 1930s, when Tarski proposed his definition of truth, there was similar skepticism about such extensional concepts as truth and denotation. Many scientifically inclined philosophers (for example, Carnap and Neurath among others) believed that truth was a metaphysical concept devoid of empirical content. It seemed to them that any attempt to define truth involved metaphysical notions—for example, "reality" in "truth is correspondence with reality." They argued that any attempt to define truth in terms of empirical concepts is bound to fail, for empirical observations never justify our claim to know that such and such is *true* but only that it is probable or well confirmed. Further, many of these philosophers, perhaps as a result of their skepticism, believed that the concept of truth was not really needed for scientific purposes. All the ends that seemed to be served by the concept of truth, they argued, could equally well be served by other more empirically respectable concepts such as "verified", "confirmed", and "probable".

It was in this context that Tarski proposed his definition of truth. He argued that truth was a useful concept for certain branches of science and for the methodology of science. *And he proved that truth could be defined purely in terms of logical and empirical concepts, and hence he showed that the empiricist skepticism about this concept was unjustified* (Tarski (1944), (1956a), (1956b)). More accurately, Tarski showed that the concept "is-a-true-sentence-of-L" could be defined in a suitably rich metalanguage using only the concepts of L, concepts of the morphology of L, and the logical concepts. In particular, the definition of truth employs no undefined semantic concept such as denotation or satisfaction (unless some such concept already belongs to L). It is thus that Tarski made truth a scientifically respectable notion; and his achievement was recognized by philosophers at the time. Popper wrote some years later, "Thanks to Tarski's work, the idea of objective or absolute truth—that is truth as correspondence with facts[13]—appears to be accepted today with confidence by all who understand it" (Popper (1965) p. 224).

It must be emphasized that Tarski did not attempt a "physicalistic" reduction of the concept of truth. Field (1972) has drawn a parallel between Tarski's attempt to reduce semantic concepts to nonsemantic ones and the attempts by various physicalists to reduce, for example, concepts of chemistry to physical concepts. This parallel is not very

13. Although Tarski also claims that his theory is a correspondence theory of truth, this is doubtful. The point I am making does not rely on it.

good. (A better parallel to draw would be between Tarski's definition of truth and the Frege–Russell definition of number. But this has its shortcomings, too.) There are many reasons why Field's analogy fails. One major reason is that in scientific reductions such as the one of "valency" to physical concepts there is no attempt to preserve meaning or sense of the original expression. This was, however, Tarski's intention. In a word, Tarski was attempting to carry out an "analytical" reduction of the concept of truth, not a "physicalistic" reduction.[14]

How far did Tarski succeed in this project? I believe that he succeeded in showing that the concept of truth for certain languages L can be defined analytically in an essentially richer metalanguage ML, *when ML contains L.* For here it is plausible to claim that the T-biconditionals are "partial definitions of truth"; that they explain the sense of expressions of the type 'the sentence x is true in L'. This is plausible because in this special case the biconditionals are analytically true. We know simply in virtue of the meanings of the words that sentences such as

'Snow is white' is true (in English) if and only if snow is white

cannot be false. Moreover the definition of 'true-in-L' is in a sense nothing more than a logical sum of all these analytically true T-sentences. Hence it seems to me that Tarski has some claim to have shown that for certain L's and certain ML's, 'true-in-L' can be analytically defined in ML.

This argument does not apply when ML does not contain L. The biconditionals now are not analytically true. Still, 'true-in-L' can be defined *if we allow the use of the concept of translation in the definition* and if ML is essentially richer in its conceptual resources. Now there

14. There is much evidence for this in Tarski's writings. For example, he says about the T-biconditionals that

> Statements of this form can be regarded as partial definitions of the concept of truth. They explain in a precise way, and in conformity with ordinary usage, the sense of all special expressions of the type: *the sentence x is true* (Tarski (1956b) p. 404).

And about the definition of truth he says,

> it will fulfill what we intuitively expect from every definition; that is, it will explain the meaning of the term being defined in terms whose meaning appears to be completely clear and unequivocal (Tarski (1944), section 9).

I would also suggest that the philosophical purposes to which Tarski puts his definition of truth require that he give an analytical definition.

will be a fragment of ML, say L′, which is conceptually equivalent to L and for which we can give an analytical definition of truth in ML. Now using 'true-in-L″', we can define 'true-in-L' thus:

True-in-L = Df$\{x: x$ is a sentence of L and $\exists y(y = t(x)$ and y is true-in-L′$)\}$.

(t is a translation function which maps L into L′.) I think that the above definition has some claim to be analytically true.[15]

In modal logics, too, truth can be defined under the same conditions that apply to extensional logics. More accurately, the *second* concept of truth T_2 can be explicitly defined (under proper conditions) without the use of any semantic concepts. But this is not so for the *first* concept of truth T_1. Here, only an incomplete definition is possible. A contextual definition of T_1 that does not employ semantic concepts is possible if T_1 does not occur in modal contexts. Further, if some semantic concepts are allowed, a more complete definition of T_1 can be given in certain modal logics. (See §5.) Both the explicit definition of T_2 and the contextual definition of T_1 have a claim to be analytical definitions. For the T-biconditionals

(26) 'Snow is white' is true$_1$ (in English) if and only if snow is white,

(27) 'Snow is white' is true$_2$ (in English) if and only if snow is white

are analytically true.

The analyticity of (26) and (27) has some interesting consequences which I want to note without attempting a comprehensive discussion of the issues involved. First, adequate translation functions do not always preserve analyticity. The best translation of an analytic sentence is not necessarily analytic. A good translation of (26) in French is

(28) "Snow is white" *est vrai*$_1$ *en anglais si, et seulement si, la neige est blanche*.

But whereas (26) is analytic in English, (28) clearly is not analytic in French. Second, as Thomason has pointed out, analyticity is not an attribute of some language independent entity such as propositions. Examples (26) and (28) express the same proposition, but (26) is analytic and (28) is not. In this respect, analyticity differs fundamentally from

15. Tarski's procedure does not yield an analytical definition of 'true-in-L' (i) for variable L, (ii) when L is as rich or richer than the metalanguage ML, (iii) when L has concepts not occurring in ML. (i) and (ii) do not argue against Tarski's method. In such cases it is doubtful that ML can consistently contain the concept 'true-in-L'.

necessity.[16] Third, there are analytic truths that are contingent.[17] Sentence (26) is clearly analytic, and we saw earlier that it is contingent, too. This observation reinforces our previous conclusion that there is a fundamental difference between analyticity and necessity. Fourth, in view of the analyticity of (26), sentences

(29) 'Snow is white' is true_1 (in English),

(30) Snow is white

convey the same information. Yet they express different propositions. There are worlds where (29) is true and (30) is false (and vice versa). Hence what a person says or asserts cannot be understood (even in the case of literal expression) simply in terms of the proposition his words express. Fifth, if analysis aims at analytical equivalences, then Church's translation argument (Church (1950)) rests on a false premise, namely, that if A is a good analysis of B (in L), then translation t(A) is a good analysis of t(B) (in L′). Sentences (29) and (30) convey the same information. They are analytically equivalent. Their translations in French, however, are not analytically equivalent.

An explanation of these curiosities I leave for another occasion.

§4. *Theories of Truth in Modal Logics with Sortal Quantification*

I present in this section a homophonic theory of truth for a simplified version of L_1. The main problem in constructing such theories springs from the recursive clause for □. It appears that the clause

(31) $Sat(\ulcorner\Box X\urcorner, s) \equiv \Box Sat(X, s)$

will not do when the object language is L_1. For, intuitively, the semantics of L_1 requires that to determine if *s* satisfies $\Box X$, we should shift the value of *s* (according to the appropriate principles of identity) as we move from world to world. However, (31) has no provisions for shifting the values of *s*. It seems to say that a sequence *s* satisfies $\Box X$ when and only when the sequence of *the same objects* satisfies *X* in every world.

The most obvious ways of avoiding the difficulty are unsatisfactory. We may, for example, think of satisfaction as a three-place predicate

16. We can perhaps attribute to propositions such properties as "analytic-in-English" and "synthetic-in-Finnish." (Thomason disagrees with this because he regards sentences such as 'I am here' (or their various utterances) to be analytic.) This does not go against our conclusion that analyticity, unlike necessity, is fundamentally a linguistic matter.

17. Thomason (1976) remarks on these too.

relating formulas to sequences of objects and sequences of principles of identity. Besides the various technical problems faced by this proposal (in fact, the technical problems seem insuperable to me), the method is unsatisfactory on philosophical grounds. It utilizes irreducible semantic concepts and it requires that the metalanguage be *substantially* richer than the object language. A second idea is to treat satisfaction as a relation between formulas and sequences of individual concepts. The technical problems ease on this approach, but the philosophical objection remains. A much neater solution of the problem is available. It is possible to give a homophonic truth theory for L_1 without using the idea "individual concept."

For concreteness, suppose that the object language (OL) has two common nouns K and K_1, one 1-place predicate F and one individual constant a. We suppose that OL has all the logical resources of L_1 except restriction and descriptions. We also suppose, for ease of presentation, that the common nouns of OL fulfill the condition of modal constancy (see chapter 1, §5). The metalanguage has all the resources of OL plus the following: (1) elementary arithmetic, (2) means for constructing structural descriptive names of the expressions of OL, (3) syntax of OL, (4) a two-place predicate *Sat* ("satisfaction"), (5) a one-place predicate T ("True-in-OL"), and (6) the theory of sequences presented below.

A theory of modal sequences. We solve the problem mentioned above by using an "intensional" concept of sequence. Our sequences will be sequences of K's and K_1's. At any world w, the nth value of a sequence will be a K (or a K_1) and its nth value at any other world will be the same K (or the same K_1). Thus, as we shift from world to world, the value of a sequence will also shift appropriately. These ideas are made precise in the formal theory below.

The theory of modal sequences has two primitives: one common noun *Seq* and one 3-place predicate *Val*. Intuitively, $Val(s,n,x)$ says that the value of the sequence s at the nth place is x. *Seq* and *Val* are governed by the following eight axioms. The first five axioms say, roughly, that all sequences are sequences of K's and K_1's. (In the following axioms, s,s' are understood as ranging over sequences and n,n' over natural numbers.)

Ax. 1. $\Box(\forall Seq,s)\Box\, Seq[s]$.

Ax. 2. $\Box((\exists! K,x)Val(s,n,x) \vee (\exists! K_1,x)Val(s,n,x))$.
Ax. 3. $\Box(\forall K,x)(\forall K_1,y)(Val(s,n,x) \wedge Val(s,n,y) \supset x = y)$.
Ax. 4. $\Box(\forall K,x)(Val(s,n,x) \supset$
$(\Box\, Val(s,n,x) \vee (\exists K_1,y)(x = y \wedge \Box\, Val(s,n,y))))$.
Ax. 5. $\Box(\forall K_1,x)(Val(s,n,x) \supset$
$(\Box\, Val(s,n,x) \vee (\exists K,y)(x = y \wedge \Box\, Val(s,n,y))))$.

These axioms allow us to speak of the *n*th value of a sequence. Note that we view sequences as consisting only of *K*'s and K_1's. The other values of a sequence are immaterial and can be ignored. We introduce the idea of the *n*th value of a sequence ($Val(s,n)$) via the following contextual definitions.

Df. 1. $Val(s,n) = Val(s',n') = \mathrm{Df}(\exists K,x)(Val(s,n,x) \wedge$
$Val(s',n',x)) \vee (\exists K_1,x)(Val(s,n,x) \wedge Val(s',n',x))$.
Df. 2. $Val(s,n) =^{\frown} Val(s',n') = \mathrm{Df}(\exists K,x)\Box(Val(s,n,x) \wedge$
$Val(s',n',x)) \vee (\exists K_1,x)\Box(Val(s,n,x) \wedge$
$Val(s',n',x))$.
Df. 3. $F(Val(s,n)) = \mathrm{Df}(\exists K,x)(Fx \wedge Val(s,n,x))$
$\vee (\exists K_1,x)(Fx \wedge Val(s,n,x))$.

We understand the contexts $t = Val(s,n)$ and $Val(s,n) = t$ to be defined analogously. We now state the final three axioms of the theory of sequences. Ax. 6 gives the identity conditions for sequences. Ax. 7 and Ax. 8 make certain existence claims concerning sequences.

Ax. 6. $\Box((\forall Number,n)(Val(s,n) =^{\frown} Val(s'n)) \supset s = s')$.
Ax. 7. $\Box(\exists Seq,s)Seq(s)$.
Ax. 8. $\Box(\forall K,x)(\exists Seq,s')(s \underset{n}{\doteqdot} s' \wedge \Box\, Val(s',n,x))$
$\wedge \Box(\forall K_1,x)(\exists Seq,s')(s \underset{n}{\doteqdot} s' \wedge \Box\, Val(s',n,x))$,

where $s \underset{n}{\doteqdot} s' = \mathrm{Df}(\forall Number,n')(n \neq n' \supset$
$Val(s,n') =^{\frown} Val(s',n'))$.

Theory of satisfaction and truth. The following standard axioms suffice for a theory of truth for OL.

Ax. 9. $\Box(Sat(\ulcorner Fa \urcorner,s) \equiv Fa)$.
Ax. 10. $\Box(Sat(\ulcorner Fx_n \urcorner,s) \equiv F(Val(s,n)))$.
Ax. 11. $\Box(Sat(\ulcorner a = a \urcorner,s) \equiv a = a)$.
Ax. 12. $\Box(Sat(\ulcorner a = x_n \urcorner,s) \equiv a = Val(s,n))$.
Ax. 13. $\Box(Sat(\ulcorner x_n = a \urcorner,s) \equiv Val(s,n) = a)$.
Ax. 14. $\Box(Sat(\ulcorner x_m = x_n \urcorner,s) \equiv Val(s,m) = Val(s,n))$.

Ax. 15. $\Box(Sat(\ulcorner \sim X \urcorner, s) \equiv \sim Sat(X,s))$.
Ax. 16. $\Box(Sat(\ulcorner (X \supset Y) \urcorner, s) \equiv (\sim Sat(X,s) \vee Sat(Y,s)))$.
Ax. 17. $\Box(Sat(\ulcorner \Box X \urcorner, s) \equiv \Box\, Sat(X,s))$.
Ax. 18. $\Box(Sat(\ulcorner (\forall K, x_n) X \urcorner, s) \equiv$
$(\forall K,x)(\forall Seq,s')((s' \underset{n}{\doteqdot} s \wedge \Box\, Val(s',n,x))$
$\supset Sat(A,s')))$.
Ax. 19. $\Box(Sat(\ulcorner (\forall K_1, x_n) X \urcorner, s) \equiv$
$(\forall K_1,x)(\forall Seq,s')((s' \underset{n}{\doteqdot} s \wedge \Box\, Val(s',n,x))$
$\supset Sat(A,s')))$.
Ax. 20. $T(X) \equiv (\forall Seq,s) Sat(X,s)$.

These axioms, together with standard syntactic and number theoretic axioms, imply for each closed object language sentence A, a biconditional of the form

$T(\bar{A}) \equiv A$,

where $\bar{A}$ is a structural descriptive name in the metalanguage for A. In virtue of Ax. 7 and Ax. 20, this claim is an immediate consequence of the following lemma.

Lemma. Let A be an *arbitrary* formula of OL. And let all the free variables of A occur in the list $x_{i_1}, \ldots, x_{i_n}$. Now define the formula B thus:

$$B = \text{Df } ((A^{Val(s,\bar{\imath}_1)}/x_{i_1}) \ldots)^{Val(s,\bar{\imath}_n)}/x_{i_n},$$

where s is a variable not occurring in A and $\bar{\imath}_j (1 \leq j \leq n)$ is the numeral for i_j in ML. (Note that $Val(s,\bar{\imath}_j)$ is explained away (at the jth stage) by the contextual definitions given earlier.) Now Ax. 1–Ax. 20 (with the usual syntactic and number theoretic axioms) imply for each object language sentence A

$(\forall Seq,s)\Box(Sat(\bar{A},s) \equiv B)$.

The lemma can be shown to hold by induction on the length of A. All the cases are quite straightforward except the one for the quantifier. For this case Theorem 1 is useful.

Theorem 1. Let A be a formula of ML and let $Val(s,n)$ and $Val(s',n')$ be free for the variable x in A. Then Ax. 1–Ax. 8 imply the following:

(i) $\Box(\forall K,x)(\Box\, Val(s,n,x) \supset (A \equiv A^{Val(s,n)}/x))$,
(ii) $\Box(\forall K_1,x)(\Box\, Val(s,n,x) \supset (A \equiv A^{Val(s,n)}/x))$,
(iii) $\Box(Val(s,n) =^{\cap} Val(s',n') \supset (A^{Val(s,n)}/x \equiv A^{Val(s',n')}/x))$.

§5. *Theories of Truth in Bressanian Logics*

By a Bressanian logic I understand a modal logic with intensional predication and quantification over individual concepts. (See Parks (1976) for a simple presentation of a first-order Bressanian logic.) Homophonic truth theories can be constructed in these logics in the standard way outlined above. But there is also available in Bressanian logics a somewhat different way of constructing truth theories, and this deserves mention. The method can be used to give the definition of a more general concept of truth. We can define something like the concept "the sentence x is true in a world w with the meaning it has in w′."

The method relies on the fact that in a Bressanian logic we can obtain analogues of worlds. I am indebted to Belnap and to Thomason for this observation. They have pointed out that these analogues are available in *any* Bressanian logic that meets certain minimal conditions. Let a and b be two constants that satisfy axiom

(32) $\Box a \neq b$.

We can obtain analogues of possible worlds by postulate (33) and definition (34). (The notation followed here is that of Bressan (1972).)

(33) $\Box(W(x) \equiv PR(x) \wedge (\forall y)((PR(y) \wedge \Diamond(x = y \wedge y = b)) \supset \Box(x = a \vee y = b)))$.

(34) $I(x) = \mathrm{Df}\, (W(x) \wedge (x = b))$.

PR is given the following contextual definition:

$PR(x) = \mathrm{Df}\, \Box(x = a \vee x = b) \wedge \Diamond x = a \wedge \Diamond x = b$.

W is true of all and only analogues of worlds. It can be read "is a world." *I* represents the property of being instantiated; if $x \in W$, then Ix is true in a world w iff the world represented by x is instantiated in w, that is, iff x represents w. It can be shown that *W* and *I* have most of the desired properties (see Bressan (1972) pp. 197–206). In some ways of counting, the worlds do not count right, but for the present purposes this is harmless. We record below some useful properties of *W* and *I*. (In the following theorems, $\mathbf{w}, \mathbf{w}'$ are understood to be restricted to *W*.)

(35) $\vdash \Box(\exists \mathbf{w}) I(\mathbf{w})$.

(36) $\vdash \Box A \equiv (\forall \mathbf{w}) \Box(I(\mathbf{w}) \supset A) \equiv (\forall \mathbf{w}) \Diamond(I(\mathbf{w}) \wedge A)$.

(37) $\vdash \Diamond A \equiv (\exists \mathbf{w}) \Diamond(I(\mathbf{w}) \wedge A)$.

(38) $\vdash A \equiv (\exists \mathbf{w})(I(\mathbf{w}) \wedge A) \equiv (\forall \mathbf{w})(I(\mathbf{w}) \supset A) \equiv (\forall \mathbf{w})(I(\mathbf{w}) \supset \Diamond(I(\mathbf{w}) \wedge A))$.

We now present a homophonic theory of truth for a Bressanian language. We suppose that the object language has one predicate letter F and one name a. The metalanguage contains the object language and has the usual theory of sequences (with "sequence" treated as an absolute concept), elementary arithmetic, and resources for forming structural descriptive names of the expressions of OL. Variables s,s' are understood as ranging over sequences; variables $\mathbf{w},\mathbf{w}'$, as before, over analogues of worlds. $s \underset{n}{\doteqdot} s'$ means that s and s' are identical except perhaps at the nth place.

Theory of satisfaction

(Ax. 1) $Sat(\ulcorner F(a)\urcorner, s, \mathbf{w}) \equiv \Diamond(I(\mathbf{w}) \wedge F(a))$.

(Ax. 2) $Sat(\ulcorner F(x_n)\urcorner, s, \mathbf{w}) \equiv \Diamond(I(\mathbf{w}) \wedge F(Val(s,n)))$.

(Ax. 3) $Sat(\ulcorner \sim X\urcorner, s, \mathbf{w}) \equiv \sim Sat(X, s, \mathbf{w})$.

(Ax. 4) $Sat(\ulcorner (X \supset Y)\urcorner, s, \mathbf{w}) \equiv (Sat(X, s, \mathbf{w}) \supset Sat(Y, s, \mathbf{w}))$.

(Ax. 5) $Sat(\ulcorner \Box X\urcorner, s, \mathbf{w}) \equiv (\forall \mathbf{w}')Sat(X, s, \mathbf{w}')$.

(Ax. 6) $Sat(\ulcorner (\forall x_n) Y\urcorner, s, \mathbf{w}) \equiv (\forall s')(s' \underset{n}{\doteqdot} s \supset Sat(Y, s', \mathbf{w}))$.

Theory of truth

(Ax. 7) $True(X, \mathbf{w}) \equiv (\forall s)Sat(X, s, \mathbf{w})$.

(Ax. 8) $T(X) \equiv (\exists \mathbf{w})(I(\mathbf{w}) \wedge True(X, \mathbf{w}))$.

These axioms, when conjoined with the standard axioms for sequences, *Val*, etc., imply for each closed sentence of OL a biconditional of the form (H). This is easily shown in view of theorems (35)–(38).

(H) $T(\bar{A}) \equiv A$ ($\bar{A}$ is a structural descriptive name of A).

It should be noted that the theory of truth given above determines only the extension of T; it leaves the intension of T indeterminate. We can, however, extend the theory to "define" the intension of T. This can be done in two ways, depending on whether we want a theory of truth$_1$ or a theory of truth$_2$ (see §3 above). If (Ax. 8) is strengthened to

(39) $(\Diamond(I(\mathbf{w}) \wedge T(X)) \equiv True(X, \mathbf{w}))$,

we obtain a theory of truth$_2$. We can now generate the necessitations of all the instances of (H).

We can also "define" something like the intension of truth$_1$ in a higher-order Bressanian language. Suppose that only the nonlogical constants of OL can change meaning and that they never change their logical category. Now we obtain a theory of truth$_1$ thus. We take the necessitations of (Ax. 3)–(Ax. 8) and we replace (1) and (2) by

(40) $\Box(Sat(\ulcorner F(a)\urcorner, s, \mathbf{w}) \equiv (\exists P)(\exists i)(P \in m(\ulcorner F \urcorner) \wedge i \in m'(\ulcorner a \urcorner) \wedge \Diamond(I(\mathbf{w}) \wedge P(i))))$,

(41) $\Box(Sat(\ulcorner F(x_n)\urcorner, s, \mathbf{w}) \equiv (\exists P)(P \in m(\ulcorner F \urcorner) \wedge \Diamond(I(\mathbf{w}) \wedge P(Val(s,n)))))$.[18]

P is a higher-order variable ranging over properties; i ranges over individual concepts. m and m' are the meaning functions. They give at each world the meaning (or the intension) of an expression at that world.

In the new theory, a sentence A falls in the extension of T at a world w iff A is true in w with the meaning it has in w. $True(A,\mathbf{w})$ can be interpreted thus: $\langle A,\mathbf{w}\rangle$ falls in the extension of '*True*' at a world w′ iff A is true in the world represented by **w** with the meanings it has in w′. In terms of this general concept, both concepts of truth can be defined. Also, this concept is useful in the analysis of some of our utterances, e.g.,

(42) If 'tail' had meant what 'leg or tail' means, then the sentence 'If Charlie has a leg, he has a tail' would have been necessarily true.

There is a reading of (42) on which it is true.[19] If so, then 'true' in (42) cannot be understood as expressing the first or the second concept of truth (§3). So understood, (42) is false. This sentence is most naturally analyzed using the general concept of truth defined above. It can be represented thus:

'tail' means what 'leg or tail' actually means
$\Box\!\!\rightarrow$ (**w**) *True*('If Charlie ... a tail',**w**).

18. I am indebted to Nuel Belnap for correcting an earlier, flawed version of (40) and (41).

19. Thomason has doubts about this.

Bibliography

Anderson, A. R., and Belnap, N. D. 1975. *Entailment*, vol. 1. Princeton: Princeton University Press.

Belnap, N. D. 1972. Foreword to Bressan's *A General Interpreted Modal Calculus*. In Bressan (1972).

Belnap, N. D., and Grover, D. L. 1973. "Quantifying in and out of Quotes." In Leblanc (1973).

Bressan, A. 1972. *A General Interpreted Modal Calculus*. New Haven and London: Yale University Press.

Cartwright, H. M. 1965. "Heraclitus and the Bath Water." *Philosophical Review* 74.

———. 1970. "Quantities." *Philosophical Review* 79.

Cartwright, R. 1968. "Some Remarks on Essentialism." *Journal of Philosophy* 65.

Chandler, H. S. 1976. "Plantinga and the Contingently Possible." *Analysis* 36.

Chisholm, R. M. 1967. "Identity through Possible Worlds: Some Questions." *Nous* 1.

Church, A. 1950. "On Carnap's Analysis of Statements of Assertion and Belief." *Analysis* 10.

Cresswell, M. J. 1975. "Hyperintensional Logic." *Studia Logica* 34.

Davidson, D. 1967. "Truth and Meaning." *Synthese* 17.

———. 1970. "Semantics for Natural Languages." *Linguaggi nella società e nella tecnica*. Reprinted in Davidson and Harman (1975).

———. 1973a. "In Defence of Convention T." In Leblanc (1973).

———. 1973b. "Radical Interpretation." *Dialectica* 27.

Davidson, D., and Harman, G., eds. 1975. *The Logic of Grammar*. Encino, Calif.: Dickenson.

Dummett, M. A. E. 1973. *Frege: Philosophy of Language*. London: Duckworth.

Field, H. 1972. "Tarski's Theory of Truth." *Journal of Philosophy* 69.

Frege, G. 1950. *The Foundations of Arithmetic*. Translated by J. L. Austin. Oxford: Blackwell.

Gabbay, D., and Moravcsik, J. M. 1973. "Sameness and Individuation." *Journal of Philosophy* 70.

Geach, P. 1962. *Reference and Generality*. Ithaca: Cornell University Press. (Emended edition, 1968.)

———. 1972. *Logic Matters*. Oxford: Blackwell.

Gibbard, A. 1975. "Contingent Identity." *Journal of Philosophical Logic* 4.

Griffin, N. 1977. *Relative Identity*. New York: Oxford University Press.

Harman, G. 1972. "Logical Form." *Foundations of Language* 9.

Hazen, A. 1976. "Expressive Completeness in Modal Language." *Journal of Philosophical Logic* 5.

Henkin, L. 1949. "The Completeness of the First-Order Functional Calculus." *Journal of Symbolic Logic* 14.

Hintikka, J. 1969. *Models for Modalities.* Dordrecht: Reidel.

———. 1969a. "On the Logic of Perception." In Hintikka (1969).

———. 1969b. "Semantics for Propositional Attitudes." In Hintikka (1969).

Hughes, G. E., and Cresswell, M. J. 1968. *An Introduction to Modal Logic.* London: Methuen.

Hunter, G. 1971. *Metalogic.* New York: Macmillan.

Kaplan, D. 1966. Review of Kripke (1963a). *Journal of Symbolic Logic* 31.

Kripke, S. 1963. "Semantical Considerations on Modal Logics." *Acta Philosophica Fennica* 16.

———. 1963a. "Semantical Analysis of Modal Logic I." *Zeitschrift für mathematische Logik und Grundlagen der Mathematik* 9.

———. 1972. "Naming and Necessity." In D. Davidson and G. Harman, eds., *Semantics of Natural Language.* Dordrecht: Reidel.

Lambert, K., ed. 1970. *Philosophical Problems in Logic.* Dordrecht: Reidel.

Leblanc, H., ed. 1973. *Truth, Syntax and Modality.* Amsterdam: North Holland.

Leblanc, H., and Wisdom, W. A. 1974. *Deductive Logic.* Boston: Allyn & Bacon.

Lewis, D. 1968. "Counterpart Theory and Quantified Modal Logic." *Journal of Philosophy* 65.

———. 1971. "Counterparts of Persons and Their Bodies." *Journal of Philosophy* 68.

———. 1973. *Counterfactuals.* Oxford: Blackwell.

Marcus, R. 1967. "Essentialism in Modal Logic." *Nous* 1.

Montague, R. 1974. "The Proper Treatment of Quantification in Ordinary English." In R. H. Thomason, ed., *Formal Philosophy.* New Haven and London: Yale University Press.

Parks, R. Z. 1976. "Investigation in Quantified Modal Logics I." *Studia Logica* 35.

Parsons, T. 1969. "Essentialism and Quantified Modal Logic." *Philosophical Review* 78.

Perry, J. 1970. "The Same *F*." *Philosophical Review* 79.

Popper, K. R. 1965. *Conjectures and Refutations.* London: Routledge & Kegan Paul.

Quine, W. V. O. 1950. "Identity, Ostension and Hypostasis." *Journal of Philosophy* 47. Reprinted in *From a Logical Point of View.* Cambridge, Mass: Harvard University Press, 1961.

———. 1960. *Word and Object.* Cambridge, Mass.: M.I.T. Press.

———. 1961. "Reference and Modality." In *From a Logical Point of View.* Cambridge, Mass.: Harvard University Press.

———. 1966. "Three Grades of Modal Involvement." In *The Ways of Paradox.* New York: Random House.

———. 1976. "Worlds Away." *Journal of Philosophy* 73.

Scott, D. 1970. "Advice on Modal Logic." In Lambert (1970).

Stevenson, L. 1975. "A Formal Theory of Sortal Quantification." *Notre Dame Journal of Formal Logic* 16.

———. 1977. "Extensional and Intensional Logic for Criteria of Identity." *Logique et analyse* 20.

Stalnaker, R. 1968. "A Theory of Conditionals." In *Studies in Logical Theory*, American Philosophical Quarterly Monograph Series, no. 2.

Stockwell, R. P., Schachter, P., and Partee, B. H. 1973. *The Major Syntactic Structures of English*, New York: Holt, Rinehart & Winston.

Strawson, P. F. 1954. "Particular and General." *Proceedings of the Aristotelian Society* 54. Reprinted in *Logico-Linguistic Papers*. London: Methuen, 1971.

Tarski, A. 1944. "The Semantic Conception of Truth." *Philosophy and Phenomenological Research* 4.

———. 1956. *Logic, Semantics, Metamathematics*. Oxford: Clarendon Press.

———. 1956a. "The Concept of Truth in Formalized Languages." In Tarski (1956).

———. 1956b. "The Establishment of Scientific Semantics." In Tarski (1956).

Thomason, R. H. 1969. "Modal Logic and Metaphysics." In K. Lambert, ed., *The Logical Way of Doing Things*. New Haven and London: Yale University Press.

———. 1970. "Some Completeness Results for Modal Predicate Calculi." In Lambert (1970).

———. 1973. "Perception and Individuation." In M. Munitz, ed., *Logic and Ontology*. New York: New York University Press.

———. 1976. "Necessity, Quotation and Truth." In A. Kasher, ed., *Language in Focus*. Dordrecht: Reidel.

Thomason, R. H., and Stalnaker, R. 1968. "Modality and Reference." *Nous* 2.

Wallace, J. 1965. "Sortal Predicates and Quantification." *Journal of Philosophy* 62.

———. 1970. "On the Frame of Reference." *Synthese* 22.

———. 1975. "Nonstandard Theories of Truth." In Davidson and Harman (1975).

Wiggins, D. 1967. *Identity and Spatio-Temporal Continuity*. Oxford: Blackwell.

Wittgenstein, L. 1961. *Tractatus Logico-Philosophicus*. Translated by D. F. Pears and B. F. McGuinness. London: Routledge & Kegan Paul.

Index